D16422

Wildlife
SOS

SIMON AND LOU COWELL

Wildlife
SOS

TRUE STORIES FROM
BRITAIN'S FAVOURITE ANIMAL
RESCUE CENTRE

JOHN BLAKE

Published by John Blake Publishing Ltd,
3 Bramber Court, 2 Bramber Road,
London W14 9PB, England

www.blake.co.uk

First published in hardback in 2006

ISBN-13: 978-1-84454-286-4
ISBN-10: 1 84454 286 6

British Library Cataloguing-in-Publication Data:

A catalogue record for this book is available from the British Library.

Design by www.envydesign.co.uk

Printed in Great Britain by CPI Bath

1 3 5 7 9 10 8 6 4 2

Papers used by John Blake Publishing are natural, recyclable products
made from wood grown in sustainable forests. The manufacturing processes
conform to the environmental regulations of the country of origin.

Lou

Thanks to …

Mum and Dad for Wildlife Aid; cameraman Jim (and surrogate big bro) for his memory, in lieu of my father's, as I tried to piece together the various events of the rescues featured herein; vet Andy and vet nurses Sara and Hazel, for the facts; Papa for his teachings, from which I continue to learn every day; Gem, for the hot cross buns; Chris Golsby in 'Wildlife Corner', for all manner of weird, wonderful (and often grammatically impossible) wildlife-oriented facts. Finally, thanks to all creatures great and small.

Simon

Thanks to …

Dad, who I still miss every day, but whose spirituality stays with me; Bill Alston who ignited my idea to start Wildlife Aid, and Jill for her devoted work for the charity in the early years. And the biggest possible 'thank you' to Lou, who was absolutely invaluable in helping me pull together my reminiscences of life at Wildlife Aid, and to make some sense of it all. It was Lou – daughter, singer/songwriter and now author – who turned my inane ramblings into this book. She has truly worked wonders.

Contents

Preface

by Simon's daughter
Lou Cowell

Do you know that, even with two pillows and a determined finger planted firmly over head and in ear respectively, you can still hear a phone ring?

Since moving back home to Wildlife Aid, I have grown accustomed to having my dreams punctuated by strange sirens or miscellaneous chimes as the centre's 24-hour helpline (affectionately known as 'the Bat Phone') heralds some current wildlife crisis. I often wonder whether, if I peeled open my curtains, I wouldn't see a projected image of my father's bespectacled self among the stars as his immediate presence is requested by The Animal Kingdom. In the few seconds of silence following the answered call, I can only imagine what scenario is being described: I will have to wait until morning for my own daily instalment of *Wildlife SOS*.

And so follows the familiar procedure, like a song to which I know every word: bedroom door flung open, the clumping of a staircase unceremoniously descended (twelve clumps in all – he jumps the last two steps), then the inevitable crash as he trips over our black, and therefore invisible-in-the-dark, retriever asleep at the foot of the stairs. Cursory cursing at aforementioned canine ensues, followed quickly by said canine's anthropo-morphised apology, which, in turn, is (almost) graciously accepted by my father.

Door two is then flung into dispute with its hinges; a coat is seized and thrown on – much to the detriment of anything on the surrounding surfaces; and the whirlwind that is my father has left the building, kicking up a veritable forest of leaves in his wake, which settle briefly in the utility room before starting their journey throughout the house on the breeze coming from the front door which he has left wide open. I resign myself to waking up in the Antarctic, employ the use of my third (emergencies-only) pillow, roll over and dream of bells.

Pulling the complaining wool of my jumper over my icy hands, I enter the kitchen. It's like opening the soundproofed door to a thousand-decibel gig at

Wembley: chaos and colour hit my early eyes in equal measures. One father, two cameramen, one bleary-eyed sister (whose bemused and yet acquiescent expression, I imagine, exactly mirrors my own), four dogs, cereal raining seemingly from most walls, burned toast lying dejectedly on the floor, and … one fox cub.

'Treat the earth well: it was not given to you by your parents, it was loaned to you by your children. We do not inherit the Earth from our ancestors: we borrow it from our children.'

NATIVE AMERICAN PROVERB

Deep Frees!

The Story of Hardy the Hedgehog

As I walked back to the car, trying to extract my car keys from the ever-increasing obligatory tangle of dog leads in my coat pocket, my mobile phone began growling aggressively at me, heralding a new message.

'Simon. Hedgehog in freezer. Epsom. Can you get over there?'

As I dialled the familiar sequence of digits to the centre, I momentarily imagined myself as though in some alternative universe, working undercover cracking codes and unravelling enigmas – 'The eagle has landed'; 'The hedgehog's in the freezer'! However, following a brief conversation with one of our vet nurses back at Wildlife Aid, this particular

1

mystery was, as it transpired, easily resolved: there was indeed a hedgehog.

In a freezer.

In Epsom.

Having jotted down the address, I set out on the short journey to where the prickly patient lay in wait.

Upon my arrival, I was hurriedly escorted through to a utility room and was faced with the imposing prospect of a towering freezer pulled away from the wall and straining precariously on its lead. Due to the various angles of the assorted cupboards and white goods before me, and short of hitting the room like the proverbial bomb, there was no way of creating any more leverage between freezer and wall. A very worried young lady informed me that she'd heard scratching and snuffling noises periodically throughout the morning. Evidently her partner had experienced the same strange phenomena the previous year and, after much determined (and expensive) hard graft, had managed to rescue a spiky little bundle from the toasty clutches of the freezer's compressor. Scared to leave the hedgehog where it was for the rest of the day until her husband returned from work, and not strong enough to shift the freezer any further than she had already, she'd called us.

Engaging every ounce of strength that my ageing frame would allow, I managed to extract the stubborn freezer a further precious few inches, allowing me – with the rest of my body propped haphazardly over and in between the neighbouring dishwasher and tumble dryer – to slide my arm down past the pipes and tubes to the very same compressor. At this point, a lifetime's worth of similar incidents flashed before my eyes, such as the supposed squirrel trapped behind the tank of an airing cupboard, which, in point of fact, had turned out to be a 16-foot python – an escapee from the local zoo in search of warmer climes. I instinctively retracted my arm, reliving the horror of heaving armful after armful of scaly skin – like an impossibly long chain of colourful scarves from the sleeve of a clown – careful all the while to maintain a smile that was every bit as wide and fixed as one of my circus counterpart's, so as not to alert the terrified member of the public to my utter soul-gripping phobia of snakes.

Back in the present, I drew a steady breath to strengthen my resolve, closed my eyes – the side of my head now flush against the shiny white surface, and hoped for the best. With one more indomitable stretch, my fingers brushed the unmistakable texture of muted pin cushion (spikes, not scales – a good sign). Encouraged by my find, I summoned my remaining grit, and willed my arm down further towards the little hog, while trying to close my mind to the rising heat emitted by the pipes. Success! I managed to slide my hand under the soft belly of the hog, and thus simultaneously realised that, given its size, the softness of its spines and the fact that it hadn't curled into a tight ball at my touch, this was a youngster.

Very slowly I raised my arm through the Spaghetti Junction of tubes and wires, careful to let my hand, rather than its cargo, face the scorching metal. How ironic, it occurred to me, that this little chap should crawl into the sanctuary of a freezer for warmth! Having given the hoglet a quick examination on site to check for any obvious injuries, and happy that he appeared remarkably unscathed, I wrapped him up in a towel and put him in a carry case to transport him back to the centre.

Once I was back at the hospital, our vet nurse Sara and I gave our new patient a more thorough medical. His eyes were only just open and his spines not fully sharpened, so, estimating his age to be around three to four weeks, we could only surmise that either something untoward had happened to his mother, resulting in his seeking out the protection and warmth of such a cosy hidey-hole, or he'd been unearthed by a curious dog. 'He's a hardy little guy,' Sara commented. 'Not a mark on him.'

'Hardy', as we called him, was given two-hourly

feeds (day and night) of the milk substitute that we feed to all of our youngsters, and put into an incubator with four other similarly aged orphans for company. Having been born in the first litter of the year – May–June time – he would now be kept at Wildlife Aid until September, by which stage he would have reached a suitable weight (around 600 grams) to ensure his survival through hibernation.

Come September, Hardy and his surrogate siblings were all released together, in woodland near to where Hardy was rescued.

HEDGEHOG FACT FILE

Name	Hedgehog (*Erinaceus europaeus*)
Class	Mammal
Order	Insectivora
Family	Erinaceidae
Terms	Male – boar; female – sow; young – piglet, hoglet or pup; home – nest

Distribution (globally): Hedgehogs may be found throughout the UK. (Spiny hedgehogs are also found around Africa and Eurasia.)

Habitat: They live in hedgerows, grasslands and gardens.

Size: They grow to around 25cm in length from head to tail.

Weight: Up to 2kg.

Description: Hedgehogs are usually brown and yellow in colour. Their bodies are round and bulky, with a short tail at the back. They are covered in spines, apart from their face and underside.

Lifespan
In the wild: 3 – 4 years.

In captivity: Up to 8 years. 1 human year is said to be equivalent to 10 hedgehog years.

When most commonly seen: Hedgehogs are nocturnal animals. They are seen between April and October and hibernate for the rest of the year.

Diet: They eat around 200g of food each

night, including slugs, snails, caterpillars and other insects.

Reproduction facts: Hedgehogs reach sexual maturity in their second year after birth. The ideal time for breeding is between May and June. Hedgehogs generally have two litters per year of between 4 and 6 young. The gestation period tends to last 4 weeks.

DID YOU KNOW?

Hedgehogs have been known to fight snakes. They bite the snake and roll up into a ball, repeating this procedure until the snake is dead.

There are around 6,000 spines in a hedgehog's coat!

Hedgehogs can swim, climb almost vertical walls and run at speeds of up to 2 metres per second!

A hedgehog can travel distances of 2km per night.

All Fore One

The Story of Tee the Tawny Owl

The cardboard cutout of the slick American-looking 'Hunk of Golf Pro' (Sara's sentiments, not mine), which we had spotted as we made our way towards the Golf Pro shop, moved most disconcertingly as we neared the shop's entrance.

Mistakenly assuming that the door, which had been so chivalrously swung open for Sara (by one somewhat suspiciously name-badged 'Chad'), would remain as such for my entrance, I distributed the weight of the equipment I was carrying between both hands – a decision that I immediately regretted, as the heavy sprung door swung back in my face, sending me and the aforementioned paraphernalia flying.

9

A few moments later, as I struggled into the shop with my precariously reassembled cargo, I found 'Chad', clearly oblivious to my plight, earnestly filling Sara in on the story of how he had come to have the young tawny owl, which Sara was examining on the makeshift surface of the shop's counter, in his possession.

Between us, Sara and I quickly determined that the young tawny owl was in good health. The next question was: would we be able to get it back to its mother? By now, 'Chad' had veered smoothly off the subject of his claimed heroism, and was fast plotting a new course in the direction of his own spectacular golfing achievements. Steering him, in no uncertain terms, sharply back around, I asked, 'Do you remember exactly where on the fairway you found him?' 'Chad' was visibly stumped. Making his excuses, he sloped off into a little room at the side of the shop floor, whereupon a muffled conversation took place, resulting in the triumphant re-emergence seconds later of one 'Chad', memory seemingly miraculously restored. 'The twelfth green,' he announced through a glare of teeth whiter than the row of brand-new golf balls stacked neatly behind him.

Before I knew it, the three of us were sandwiched together haphazardly on a golf buggy, 'Chad' at the wheel, with me, at Sara's discreet insistence by virtue of a sharp shove, next to him, and Sara herself to my right. I wasn't entirely sure that the speed at which 'Chad' was chauffeuring us was entirely necessary; nor was I convinced I could see the various obstacles in our path that required him to exercise his dubious repertoire of rally-esque manoeuvres.

Five minutes later, with a combination of my lunch and adrenalin coursing through my system, we finally arrived at the twelfth green, where, for the half-hour that followed, we scoured every inch of the fairway. Splitting up, Sara and I thoroughly scanned both the branches and the craggy grass bases of the trees, rooted through the undergrowth (for tawny owls are among the few birds of prey that will nest on the ground), and searched every nook and cranny of hedgerow in the area, eyes peeled for any evidence at all of owl inhabitancy – namely droppings or pellets (the waste product regurgitated by an adult owl following every meal, comprising all the indigestible parts, such as feather and bone, of its prey). Our investigation was not aided in the slightest by the continual hollers of *'Fore!'* immediately preceding each round of golf-ball fire, which I managed to avoid, but Sara, as if summoned by the call, proved an uncanny target for!

With no sign whatsoever of the parents, Sara now black and blue, and a young tawny owl far too young to be left out alone, we decided it better that we head back to the centre. So, collecting the owlet in the cardboard box that 'Chad' had provided, Sara and I set off for the comforting golf-ball-free zone of the centre.

Once safely inside the Intensive Care Unit, 'Tee', now thus called, was, thereafter, fed on a diet of chopped chick and mouse every three hours, guzzling vast portions at each sitting, consuming far more than an adult tawny, to aid the rapid growth that would take him from just out of the egg to full-sized in only fourteen weeks, and lead to his being renamed 'Mr Tee'.

One of the more hardy species of owl, the young tawny progressed resiliently through Wildlife Aid's rehabilitation plan – from ICU to second hospital, second hospital to fox pen (an outdoor enclosure that would allow him to acclimatise to the various weather conditions, but stay dry) and from fox pen to hacking house, where he stayed for just shy of a month in the company of three other tawny owls of a similar age.

The hacking houses are the final stage of the centre's rehabilitation process. These aviaries are specifically designed so that birds of prey can see their surrounding area, but not the people involved in their care. Built using breezeblocks stacked up to ten feet high, with mesh netting over the top, they have feeding tubes through which the various inhabitants' meals are passed. Again, this is designed to prevent their view of humans and so cultivate their natural instincts for a successful release into the wild.

Late one evening, around three months after we'd been there to rescue Mr Tee, Sara and I returned to the golf course with him and his three comrades (the Fairway Four) for their release. With a haunting stillness enveloping the grounds, we freed the birds from their carry case and watched their silent flight over the course.

'Four!' announced Sara.

'Indeed,' I laughed.

TAWNY OWL FACT FILE

Name Tawny owl (*Strix aluco*)
Class Aves
Order Strigiformes
Family Strigidae

Distribution (globally): Tawny owls live across Britain and Europe and range as far south as North Africa and parts of Asia.

Habitat: Tawny owls typically live in forests, but they also inhabit trees and hedgerows in gardens, parks and farmlands. They also occasionally shelter in disused buildings and rocks.

Size: Tawny owls grow to around 35–45cm tall and have a wingspan of 90–110cm.

Weight: Females weigh slightly more than males. Males range from about 400 to 550g, while females tend to be between 550 and 700g.

Description: Tawny owls have a reddish brown coat, with grey, brown and black streaks. They have round faces, with large, deep-set black eyes.

Lifespan
In the wild: The oldest wild bird is thought to have been 19 years old.
In captivity: Up to 23 years.

When most commonly seen: Tawny owls are nocturnal, so are usually seen only at night, all year round.

Diet: They mainly eat small mammals, small birds, fish and insects.

Reproduction facts: Tawny owls pair up for life. They form territories in the autumn, and the female begins to lay eggs between March and April. The incubation period lasts up to 30 days, as the eggs are laid at intervals and hatch at different times. The chicks are fully fledged after about 35 days.

DID YOU KNOW?
The distinctive call heard at night is actually a duet. The male makes the 'twit' sound, and the female the 't-woo'.

Tawny owls locate their prey by sound. They turn their heads slowly to pinpoint the prey by ear.

Tawny owls are exceptional hunters – they are even capable of catching bats in mid-flight.

Oh Deer

The Story of Felix
the Fawn

I stared at him and he stared at me, as though each silently daring the other to make his move. And then, in the merest blink of an eye, the young deer shot off in the direction of an adjoining field, with me in calculated pursuit.

I had been summoned – while en route with vet nurse Hazel to accomplish some Wildlife Aid related errand – by a call from the hospital, which had resulted in a sharp about-turn, following a lightning-quick stock-take of the boot's contents. Net? Check. Blankets? Check. Carry case? Check.

The volunteers back at the centre had already asked the vital questions of the member of the public who had alerted us to the youngster's plight,

ascertaining that the fawn had indeed been abandoned, and wasn't just awaiting its mother's return. (The doe will often leave her young for anything up to eight hours at a time, so, provided the fawn isn't wet or cold and bedraggled, we advise that people not intervene unnecessarily.)

This particular youngster had been unknowingly observed by our worried caller for nearly six and a half hours and, having seemed quite content initially, was beginning to show distinct signs of distress. In addition, the setting sun was beckoning the cold weather in for the night, so time was now of the essence.

Approaching a suspiciously wire-clad section of fence, I (for reasons now completely beyond me, and in a fit of what I can only surmise was misguided assumed youth) decided that, rather than put a provisional hand out first, I would just go for broke and throw both caution and one age-defying fifty-year-old leg to the wind – and over the collection of wood and wire. The string of jumbled sounds that followed this ill-considered whim I could, responsibly, no more type than spell. The fence was electric. And so, I was told by onlookers – who presumably were judging by my expression – were parts of me that I didn't even know existed before that moment.

The fawn, now halfway across the paddock,

turned and paused as if laughing smugly under its breath at the spectacle in its wake.

Once safely over the obnoxious fence, the young deer and I orbited one another once more. I edged slowly closer, locked in the fawn's gaze, until, just yards from the little one, I became very still.

'Become the animal,' I repeated in my head, over and over again. This is what I tell new volunteers at Wildlife Aid when teaching them how to approach just such situations. 'Think how the animal thinks; see through its eyes.'

Crouching down almost imperceptibly slowly so as to become level with the fawn's slight stature, I did just that. The fawn was scared; I did my best to become empathically aware of its fear. Two or three times over the next few minutes, I backed away from the youngster to allow it to calm down. As its darting eyes frantically sought out the best escape route, I looked away, keeping tabs on it through the corner of my eye, as I too rapidly surveyed all possible paths that could aid its hasty getaway.

Time passed – each second seemingly a lethargic hour in duration. And then, in an instant signalled by a silent starter pistol, like synchronised athletes we both lurched to the left and tumbled to the ground, with me taking the brunt of the fall, and, in doing so, acting as a cushion for the fawn's landing.

Though the fawn jerked and scrambled in my arms, I tried to remain as still as I could.

Under normal circumstances I'm sure anybody else, on seeing a grown man fly ten feet through the air only to be met by something of a nasty 'thud' as he hit the floor, would run in a panic to his side. Not Hazel though. Having witnessed several of my just such ungainly flight paths before, she calmly collected the carry case and blankets from the car and made her way over to us, stopping just short of the scene, awaiting my signal.

By now, I was sitting cross-legged on the grass with the fawn lying cradled in my arms. The youngster had ceased struggling and, instead, rested serenely in my lap as though under a trance. I quietly spoke to it in soothing tones to try to maintain its stillness. Without even daring to risk a glance in Hazel's direction as she approached, I nodded my head indicating that she should bring the carry case to me.

As soon as we arrived back at the centre, Hazel and I checked the young animal over thoroughly. Based on its size, and the fact that its umbilical cord was still attached, we assumed it to be just two or three days old. Rehydration fluids were administered immediately, owing to the fact that it had been away from its mum for so long, to combat dehydration – the fluid was warmed first so it wouldn't be too much of a shock to the youngster's system.

Taking on the role of surrogate mother to 'Felix', Hazel hand-reared the youngster, initially on a diet of colostrum (the nutrient-rich, antibody-packed first product of a new mother's breasts prior to the production of true milk), and then a specially developed milk substitute.

Letting the healthy young deer go – when the time came for it to begin the centre's Soft Release Programme – was heartbreaking for Hazel. But seeing him eventually run free back to his kind would be proof enough for her that she had played her part.

Once Felix was four weeks old, Hazel drove him down to the home of some friends of Wildlife Aid, Chris and Sylvia, a very caring retired couple, who would be able to devote all of their time to the growing fawn, continuing its bottle feeding for a further ten weeks, before introducing it to 'browse' (the name given to the leaves and foliage etc that make up their natural diet). Then Felix would start to live outside in a very large enclosure within their garden. Away from roads and people and backing on to a forest, this would be the perfect release site for the youngster when the time came.

OH DEER

After many weeks of his being outside, human contact with Felix was slowly broken and, in due course, the door to his large pen was left open, allowing the young deer to explore his territory at his own pace. Felix gradually began to venture further and further afield until his return visits to the pen in Chris and Sylvia's garden became fewer and further apart, before finally ceasing completely. Two years later, though, Felix can still be seen stopping in for a quick munch on Sylvia's prizewinning roses – much to her mock irritation!

Every Rose has its Fawn

The Story of Petal, Rose's Fawn

Rose's story will stay with me for all my days.

Of all the creatures we treat here at Wildlife Aid, deer are the hardest. Fawns are the heartbreakers, so fragile are they and, like their parents, so painfully prone to stress. Rose's story began late one spring evening.

The police car swung into the driveway of the twilit centre, triggering the floodlights to illuminate further the anxious faces of the police officers as they stepped out of their vehicle and made their way towards where I was waiting to greet them.

'She's been quiet all the way here,' one informed me. 'Barely stirred. It's a miracle she's still alive. I've never seen one hurt so bad and still breathing.'

As I gingerly opened the boot, my eyes were filled with horror at the sight that confronted them. Half covered by a blanket, the doe lay in a contorted spasm of pain, her whole body tensed and rigid, every muscle desperately trying to hang on to life. Blood covered her face – one side of which was, literally, missing – and bubbled from her mouth, ears and nose. She'd been hit head-on by a car. I nestled in beside her and, hardly daring to breathe, peeled back the blanket only to reveal the very thing that I had most feared: she was heavily pregnant.

With the help of the visibly choked officers, I carried the deer up to one of our deer sheds and laid her on a bed of fresh straw. By this time, she had started to throw her head back between her shoulder blades – a behaviour recognised by all who work here at the centre as the creature's death throes. Administering immediate antishock treatment and painkillers, I decided that all I could do was pray. I prayed for time and I prayed for a miracle. As it transpired, I got just enough of the former to allow for the latter.

Realising how advanced her labour had been, I had called in our vet, Andy. Upon his arrival, Andy had quickly confirmed my impending fear: there was no alternative but to put an end to her suffering. Her injuries were just too extensive for her to be saved. Andy immediately anaesthetised

27

Rose, and the two of us set about gently easing the fawn's frail front legs from within her.

A short while later, Rose's fawn lay at her sleeping mother's side before us. Checking that the newly born youngster was breathing for herself, that her nose was clear of birth fluid, Andy took the heartrending step of euthanising Rose (by way of an injection into her leg) before she could come round from her anaesthesia and realise her unbearable pain.

We were now faced with the daunting task of hand-rearing the orphaned youngster ourselves. Because fawns are extremely highly strung and therefore notoriously difficult to treat, it has been the practice of Wildlife Aid for some years now that one person 'adopt' each of the orphans, acting as a surrogate mother, so that the nominated foster parent is with the fawn 24/7, feeding it and caring for it to such an extent that the fawn sleeps either on or beside the foster parent's bed. Without the bond of a mother's love, these delicate souls rarely survive.

Inwardly cringing at the late hour, I called our head veterinary nurse, Sara, who, dutifully (and slightly dishevelled), arrived twenty minutes later.

It is imperative that young deer receive colostrum from their mother for the first three or four days following their birth, so, in this instance, Sara would have the fawn suckling from a bottle of substitute goats' colostrum every two hours. As the little one grew stronger, the colostrum would be replaced by Ovilac – a milk substitute – until the fawn was ready to be introduced to 'browse', which it would be slowly weaned on to entirely over a course of six or seven months. In the wild, young deer can stay with their mothers for up to a year.

Sara and her four-legged charge formed a powerful bond, and, with her love, the fawn grew strong and proud.

Many months later, her sleek coat blending seamlessly into the golden-brown leaves that autumn had bestowed, 'Petal', as Sara had named the fawn, was becoming restless, as though silently yearning for her own kind – glimpsed only in the most distant field of her memory.

Having charted events from the night of Rose's arrival, and right the way through Petal's sometimes clumsy, and yet, somehow, always graceful journey into adulthood, Sara and I set out with the Wildlife SOS crew to release Petal back into the wild.

With the unmistakable, comforting aroma of autumn floating gently around us, as the setting sun softly sang its final chorus to the waiting moon, Petal stood still, senses dancing wildly, just yards from Sara and me. Moving towards her, Sara reached out and tapped her soft rump encouragingly. As is the way with most of our deer releases, Petal needed a little prompting to forgo our now familiar ways for those that her instinct craved. Her head turned to Sara one last time – a silent 'thank you'.

As, step by step, she slowly entered the wild, darkness was beginning to descend. Suddenly, from nowhere, a herd of wild horses appeared from the failing light. Sara and I, breath held, looked on in total awe of the scene that was unfolding before us, the only sound audible being the muted whirr of the camera behind us.

One of the horses, breathing heavily and tossing its mane into the night sky as it nodded its head purposefully, began to walk forward to where our innocent youngster stood.

Halting at Petal's side, the gentle equine giant dwarfed her humble frame. Lowering her head, in a maternal expression of welcoming, the mare wound her neck protectively around Petal's, shifting her position only slightly, moments later, to lick the side of the young deer's face.

The herd moved slowly into the night together.

Turning to our cameraman, I noticed that his camera, rather than weighing down one shoulder, was resting on the ground between his feet. Still fixed in an expression of sheer wonder, he wordlessly gestured to me that the tape had stopped.

Watching Petal's return to freedom, so, for a moment there, had my heart.

ROE DEER FACT FILE

Name	Roe deer (*Capreolus capreolus*)
Class	Mammal
Order	Artiodactyla
Family	Cervidae
Terms	Male – stag; female – doe; young – fawn

Distribution (globally): Roe deer can be found in most parts of Europe and Asia. They are, however, absent in Ireland and large parts of Britain.

Habitat: Roe deer typically live in woodlands and grassy valleys.

Size: They grow to about 100–130cm in length, and 60–70cm tall (to shoulder).

Weight: 20–30kg.

Description: The coats of roe deer can be a variety of colours, depending on the time of year, from red to brown to black. They have white patches on their backside and chin. They have short antlers, growing up to only

25cm. Fawns are born with lots of white spots, which they lose with age.

Lifespan
In the wild: 10–12 years (average).
In captivity: Can live to over 20 years.

When most commonly seen: Roe deer can be active throughout the 24-hour period, but the main peaks of activity occur at dawn and dusk.

Diet: They are quite fussy eaters, choosing only the plants, shoots and grass that are most healthy.

Reproduction facts: Roe deer mate around July and August. The gestation period lasts about 9 months, which includes a 4-month period when there is no embryonic growth, then a 5-month period of foetal development. The female usually gives birth to 1–2 fawns of opposite sexes. They are born the following spring and, although weaned within 10 weeks, may stay with their parents for up to a year.

DID YOU KNOW?

Roe deer's antlers grow in the winter and are shed in the autumn.

Roe deer became extinct in England in the eighteenth century before being reintroduced.

Both male and female roe deer are solitary animals and are also very territorial.

Jewels in the Crown

The Story of Ruby
the Magpie

The three of us stood hunched at the bar, hands wrapped tightly around steaming coffee cups. Matt, Goff and I had been on (and at times in) the rough waters of a Horsham lake for the best part of the morning trying to round up an unruly squadron of orphaned ducklings, and were now trying to elevate our consequent baseline body temperatures with the caffeinated offerings of one Mrs Daisy Miller, landlady of the waterside's local establishment, The Crown.

Mrs Daisy (as she preferred to be known) had opened up the pub's doors especially for us, having followed our morning's escapades through the upstairs window, beckoning us in amid the

tantalising aromatic clouds of freshly ground coffee.

Stationed by the fireplace was, I assumed, Mr Miller. It was hard to tell at a glance where the well-lived-in armchair ended and he began. I extended a gestured greeting to him across the empty pub. Nothing. 'Don't mind him, love, blind as a bat, deaf as a post!' chortled Mrs Daisy.

Settling around one of the small, distinctly haphazard, round tables, we three bedraggled duckling captors, joined by our hospitable landlady, sat back to let our frozen spirits thaw (aided, I quietly suspected, by the covert contribution of a certain 'special ingredient' to our coffees).

Mrs Daisy was the stuff of nursery rhymes: a ruddy-cheeked, apron-clad storyteller of the highest order. Lulled by her soothing tones, I leaned back in my chair as she cast stories of The Crown's history, along with that of the local area in general, over us. Drawing out particular parts of her tale with her hands for emphasis, she would each time absent-mindedly touch her left ear, leading me to notice that it was bare of the large sparkling earring that adorned her right lobe. I smiled, inwardly conceding that it only added to her scatty charm. As if reading my thoughts, she said, 'Expect you think I'm losing my marbles, don't you?' She brushed the missing earring's site as she said this.

'I, uh …' I reached unsuccessfully for the words.

'I must be,' she laughed. 'I'm an earring short on four pairs: an engagement ring, and he' – she motioned towards a sleeping, questionably unconscious Mr Miller – 'seems to have *misplaced* his Sunday-best cufflinks and the hinge from one side of his spectacles.' They did appear wonky now I looked.

'The joys of old age,' she concluded simply with a smile.

Launching straight back into the specifics of 1950s Horsham, she continued. I, however, was becoming increasingly distracted by an intermittent high-pitched, digital-sounding 'beep' detectable primarily due to its lack of harmony with such an olde-worlde, country-pub environment.

Once again she paused in her storytelling to answer my unspoken query. 'Smoke alarm needs a *new battery*!' She threw out the last two words at ear-splitting volume, causing Mr Miller to stir, which, I gathered from the trajectory of her now rolling eyes, was the desired effect.

The more I focused in on the supposed failing smoke alarm, the more suspicious of it I became. For one, it was distinctly irregular; and, for two, its pitch and duration were inconsistent – neither being particularly indicative of a 'digital technology' fault.

Leaving Matt and Goff enraptured in an

admirably animated account of the demise of barge traffic in the sixties, I wandered over in the direction of the beeping. Ruling out Mr Miller as a possible source, I took a few steps further in the direction of the fireplace. The closer I got, the more the beeps seemed to turn into cheeps. I was intrigued.

As I reached up into the bow above the fireplace, my hand quickly located what felt like the underside of a foliage-constructed nest.

Ten minutes later, with the help of Mrs Daisy's compact handbag mirror and Matt's agility, we had before us a slightly charcoaled collection of twigs and leaves, a soot-covered magpie, four earrings, one engagement ring and one spectacle hinge.

We could only speculate as to the original circumstance of our current finding. Could the nest have fallen from a higher point in the chimney? Had the parents taken flight at the lighting of the fire below? Or had they been the victims of some other misfortune – a cat, the road, perhaps? The lone young magpie seemed thin. I could feel her keel (breastbone) protruding sharply through the juvenile plumage of her chest. I'd felt worse, but was in no doubt that the youngster had been at least a couple of days without nourishment. Given the situation, whatever the initiating factors, I was stunned at this young bird's resilience.

Mrs Daisy hurried to produce a box containing a fresh tea towel from the pub's kitchen to serve as a carry case for their unexpected visitor, into which I carefully placed 'Ruby'.

By emptying the rest of the nest (magpies are notorious thieves), we had inadvertently reclaimed the Millers' proverbial lost marbles, much to our collective bemusement. I'd been called out to numerous smoke and burglar alarms posing as nestlings before now, but never the reverse scenario!

Leaving Mr Miller (with his new re-centred vision) fumbling with the wrongly accused smoke alarm and a new nine-volt battery, Mrs Daisy walked us out to the car, wishing us well and insisting we pay her a visit next time we were passing.

Much to her displeasure, Ruby was given a 'shower' as soon as she arrived at the hospital. Using washing-up liquid and warm water, Sara carefully rinsed the soot from the young magpie's feathers and then gave her a dose of kaolin in case, prior to its removal, she had ingested any of the soot upon trying to preen herself. Force-fed with chick and cat food for the next few days until her weight was as it should be, Ruby was then put into one of the centre's small aviaries to practise the art of flight before being successfully released into the wild a couple of weeks later.

MAGPIE FACT FILE

Name	Magpie (*Pica pica*)
Class	Aves
Order	Passeriformes
Family	Corvidae

Distribution (globally): Magpies inhabit most of Britain, much of Europe, Asia, North Africa and areas of North America.

Habitat: Magpies live in open woodlands, suburban parks, gardens and farmlands.

Size: Magpies grow to about 40–45cm in body length, with a wingspan of 45–55cm and a tail length of around 20cm.

Weight: Male (average): 200–240g; female (average): 150–200g.

Description: The magpie has a very distinctive black and white plumage, with iridescent feathers that shine green and blue in the light. They have long tails, the male's tail tending to be longer than the female's.

Lifespan: Maximum 21 years, although this is unlikely in the wild due to both natural and manmade hazards.

When most commonly seen: All year round.

Diet: Magpies are omnivorous. They eat insects, beetles, seeds and fruit. They will also raid other birds' nests for eggs and nestlings, and will scavenge on small dead mammals.

Reproduction facts: Magpies reach sexual maturity after 2 years. The breeding season is between April and June. The female tends to lay only one brood. However, sometimes, if this brood fails, she will lay another. There are about 5–7 eggs in a normal brood, and the eggs take 18 days to hatch. The young are fledged in about 4 weeks.

DID YOU KNOW?

Magpies often ride on animals' backs, to feed on ticks.

Magpies are notorious thieves, often taking brightly coloured objects from gardens.

In some areas, magpies are associated with the devil. Superstitious people still, to this day, cross themselves or salute upon seeing a magpie.

Number 5: Alive!

The Story of Number 5
the Cygnet

This was more like it. Gone were the soaring temperatures (and thus 'ripe' summer aromas) of the hospital, which was filled with its usual array of incubators generating heat necessary for the youngsters, despite the searing sun of a mid-August afternoon such as this. Instead, the delicious summer heat drifted past me, diluted by a gentle breeze, as we travelled on a boat down the Thames.

Glancing down at the innocent little bundle of cygnet cradled in my arms, I recollected her story so far. Following a phone call from a member of the public, telling me that they had found the youngster trapped between a building and some panelling, I had jumped straight in the car, asking them to put it

in a box and keep it dark, quiet and out of the sun until I could get there.

No sooner had I arrived at the dock than said box was thrust firmly into my hands. Not knowing what to expect, I had been pleasantly surprised to find a bright-eyed, seemingly healthy young cygnet looking up at me expectantly. Scooping her up, I checked her over for any signs of injury or illness. Finding nothing, my thoughts immediately turned to the whereabouts of the rest of her family. I could glean nothing from the rapidly increasing crowd that had swiftly begun to form around me. Filming *Wildlife SOS* has taught me that there's nothing like a couple of TV cameras to draw a crowd, as one such 'neck-craner' found to his cost: out of the corner of my eye, I had spotted him a moment earlier hauling himself back on to the jetty from the water!

Although there were mutterings as to the presence of several mute swans in the area, there was no mention at all of nesting pairs or cygnets. I had thought I was left with no alternative but to take the orphan back to the centre. However, just in the nick of time, a gentleman had forced his way to the front of the onlookers with just the words I wanted to hear.

'I think I know where the parents are.'

He had my full attention.

'There's a pen and cob nesting just downstream from here with five cygnets. Well,' he corrected himself, 'there *were* five – the last couple of days there's just been the four. We thought maybe a fox had taken the fifth, but seeing this little 'un – she's the same size and everything – I think she's the missing link.'

'Can you take us to them?' I asked.

And so, after I'd paused briefly to lower the cygnet into the water – where I held her weight for a short time while she drank and cooled down from the day's heat – 'Number 5' and I had set sail.

In no time we were disembarking just metres away from the family of swans, who, paddling near to the bank feeding on titbits from an elderly couple, were just as my newly acquired guide, Michael, had stated: cob, pen and four cygnets. Glancing between the happily bobbing quartet of youngsters just ripples away, and the cygnet in my hand, I felt sure that Number 5 was, well, Number 5.

Staying just far enough away from the protective parents and their young so as not to spook them, but close enough for Number 5 to have them clearly in her sights and be able to swim across to them, I knelt down by the water's edge, and lowered her into the river. The instant her downy body touched the surface of the cool water, she was off on an undeterred course for her family's reunion.

Michael and I looked on in delight as Number 5 nestled into her mother's side, siblings and father quickly closing in to welcome the return of their loved one. I was in no doubt that Michael had led us in the right direction.

Sitting back on the sun-dried grass of the bank, with the blissful natural sounds and scents of summer all around me, I chatted to Michael as I watched the reunited family unit of swans on the water. Five more minutes, I thought to myself – I needed to be 100 per cent assured that all was well.

Suddenly, with little warning, one of the cygnets began to drift away from the group, listless and lethargic. Her whole body just seemed to deflate before my very eyes. Number 5 was in trouble. I stood and, screening the sun with my hand, stared intently, willing her to perk up. I was faced with a difficult decision – a difficult decision that had to be made fast. The chances of finding Mum once had been remote, so I knew that locating Number 5's family a second time would be impossible. But if the cygnet's situation didn't improve rapidly she would surely perish anyway.

The instant her head began to loll lazily on to her back, I was in the water. Forgetting everything else around me, I waded towards her as quickly as the conditions would allow. Apparently dehydrated and sun-weak, the youngster appeared unable to support even the weight of her own head. I had to get her back to the centre. Immediately.

Number 5's first 24 hours at Wildlife Aid were crucial. Under careful surveillance in the hospital's ICU, however, the youngster slowly started to recuperate. Once we were confident she was feeding on her own, Number 5 was introduced to the family of orphaned ducklings with whom she would spend the rest of the Wildlife Aid rehabilitation process. Accepting her into their fold automatically – even if she did stand head and shoulders above them! – her adoptive family allowed her the benefit of growing up amid her own(ish!) webbed kind, rather than alone with sporadic human intervention – which is always a far more preferable option to us here at the centre. The young ducklings took to her as something of a 'big sister' or, indeed, 'au pair' over time, flocking around her on colder days, and looking up to her when the day came for their first Nursery Pond outing.

Number 5 was successfully released, with her new family, into a nearby colony of immature wild mute swans three months later.

SWAN FACT FILE

Name	Mute swan (*Cygnus olor*)
Class	Aves
Order	Anseriformes
Family	Anatidae
Terms	Male – cob; female – pen; young – cygnet

Distribution (globally): Swans are found throughout Britain and Europe; they also live in some parts of Australasia, Asia, South Africa and North America.

Habitat: Swans inhabit a variety of waters, including lakes, reservoirs, canals, rivers, ponds and sheltered coasts.

Size: Swans grow to about 140–160cm in length and have a wingspan of 220–240cm.

Weight: Females tend to be slightly lighter than males, but swans can weigh up to 20kg.

Description: The mute swan is the largest of Britain's birds. They have white feathers, with long, slender necks. They have an orange bill

with black parts underneath and around the
nostrils. The area between the bill and the
eyes is featherless and forms a black lump
called a 'cere' which is commonly larger on
males. Cygnets are a light grey colour, with
grey bills.

Lifespan
In the wild: Usually 5–15 years.
In captivity: Can live up to 50 years.

When most commonly seen: Swans are seen
all year round.

Diet: Mute swans are mainly vegetarian,
eating aquatic plants, grain and grasses.
However, they do occasionally eat insects and
small fish.

Reproduction facts: Swans become sexually
mature after 3 or 4 years. It is commonly
believed that swans pair up for life. However,
this is not necessarily true. Mute swans mate
during March and April. Both the male and
female build the nests, which are situated close
to the water and are often used year after year.

A typical brood consists of 5–7 eggs, which are laid at 48-hour intervals. The female incubates the eggs for about 34–38 days, though the male does take over at times. The cygnets then often stay with the parents until the winter.

DID YOU KNOW?

Mute swans are not actually mute. They do make some noises, such as hisses.

An adult swan can eat up to half its weight (4kg) a day in vegetation.

Swans can fly at speeds of up to 88kph (55mph).

Swans ingest grit to help them to digest their food.

David and Goliaths

The Story of David the Duckling
(and Family)

Spirits at the centre were in fine fettle. The summer, following its seasonal hibernation, was yawning, stretching and youthfully enveloping Wildlife Aid's every nook and cranny in glorious warm sunshine. Feeling a little like the Pied Piper, as I strolled back down to the office followed by my 'shadow' (comprising of three dogs, four geese and one fawn), having completed my morning rounds of the centre, I began to wonder what the day would bring. As it turned out, the answer to my unposed question came just moments later in the form of a humble yellow Post-it note:

Simon.

5 Ducklings.

Big lake. Take backup!
Sara.

Right. Ducklings. Time to round up the troops. I made a couple of calls to two of the centre's most experienced rescuers, and within the hour had assembled a small but perfectly formed army of three. Loading the car with a net apiece and a carry case, we were T-minus twenty minutes, five ducklings, and counting.

This. Lake. Was. Huge. Practically an ocean for heaven's sake! Nets in hand, we three started out on a trek of its circumference – with the *Wildlife SOS* camera crew in hot pursuit, ready and only too able to capture our every blundering net-swoop for all of eternity! Halfway into our walk, I halted our procession, indicating to them with one finger to my lips to be absolutely silent.

'*Peeeeeeeeeeeeeeeeepppppp!*' Yes, there it was again. As stealthily as I could, I crept towards the water's edge in the direction of a suspiciously rustling bed of reeds. Just as I had imagined, there they were, all five, chirping to one another in hushed conspiratorial tones. I indicated the nature of my find to my fellow rescuers with a combination of pointing and five fingers held high. As quietly as I could, I extended my net to its full reach, knowing that I had only one chance at this.

WOOF, WOOF, WOOF, WOOF!

Just as I was about to make my move, an unwitting visitor to our scene – one hulking Alsatian dog – burst excitedly into view. As it was grappled into submission by, at the sight of our cameras, a mortified-looking owner, relative peace was temporarily restored. But the ducklings, like a Red Arrows aerial display team, had dispersed in five entirely different directions across the murky water.

Time to call in the troops. With a quick apologetic glance down at my brand-new trainers (not knowing what might be lurking on the silty floor of the lake, I couldn't afford to spare them), I hurriedly rolled up my jeans and, flanked by my comrades, waded in. Time was now of the essence, as the ducklings' feathers, at such a young age, would not be waterproof, meaning that their being in the water for too long at a time could prove very dangerous indeed.

Spying two of the youngsters off to my left, I slid my net towards them underneath the water, sweeping it up as quickly as liquid gravity would allow and scooping the ducklings up in the process.

Two down. Three to go.

Having placed the pair safely in the carry case – which I had left on the bank, hoping that the babies' plaintive calls would keep their siblings from straying too far – I turned around in time to see Goff, in a complex manoeuvre involving his net, his waterlogged, billowing combat trousers and a well-timed bark from our Alsatian spectator, secure the third.

We have worked with the same camera crew now for some years, and, as far as their jobs are concerned, there is one simple rule: the animal comes first. We never re-enact a rescue or release for the sake of filming any instant involving a wild animal. They can have only as many chances to capture the moment as we do the animal in question: one.

With this in mind, seeing the fourth duckling swimming erratically over to his brothers and sisters in their unfamiliar plastic nest, our cameraman,

Jim, heroically downed his heavy camera and, reaching for the sole available receptacle to hand (his Yankees baseball cap!), he sank his leg knee-deep into the foreboding mud, from which he emerged victorious, producing the tiny duckling from his cap, like a rabbit from a hat.

Now, three men with a combined height of some 18 foot between them should be no match for one duckling (total height: 3 inches) – or so you'd think. Our final tearaway was leading us a merry dance, darting effortlessly this way and that, with an agility that our bulky frames, hampered further by severely saturated threads and tiring limbs, would not allow. I was, however, fast becoming concerned at the little one's bedraggled appearance, noticing that it was swimming ever lower in the water. There was no time to lose. It was all hands on deck. So, both cameraman and soundman downed their equipment, rolled up their jeans and joined us in the water.

Between the five of us, we formed a semicircle fenced with outstretched arms, and very slowly walked the duckling in towards the bank. Torn between the calls of his family and his fear of us, the forlorn little soul paddled uncertainly, pausing every few seconds as if in some kind of trance, and tilting his head to one side – a known sign of distress. This was very bad news.

At this tender age, ducklings, because they can't self-regulate their body temperature, can't be away from Mum for too long. They need to punctuate each period of time in the water with a spell of sitting beneath her for warmth. Their predators are many, including birds such as herons and crows, either of which will swoop down and pick them off without a moment's hesitation. Pike will also snatch up any of the youngsters who are trailing too far behind their mother, as will snakes and foxes.

Helped by the barrier of Goff's net, I was able to scoop the fading youngster into my own.

Even with the heat of a willing July sun beating down upon us, I knew we must get our charges back to the hospital and under an infrared light without delay.

With a standard supermarket mop head for a 'Mum', the two-day-old ducklings were kept in a heated incubator for five weeks. After this time, they were moved into the centre's second hospital, where they were given slightly less heat, thus allowing them to acclimatise, along with a large tray of water to swim in. Finally, two weeks later, the young ducks were relocated to the top pond, where they had free access to water in order to get all of their waterproofing present and correct. Once they were ready, and fully waterproof, the ducks were released back to their ocean (lake).

Out of the Fishing Line, into the Fire!

The Story of Blaze the Duckling

If ducklings are going to get themselves into trouble, why, just once, can't it be on a small pond or, better still, a puddle? Why must these tiny souls always face their demons on such gargantuan lakes?

I stared out at the massive body of water before me, magnified a further daunting ten times by the binoculars through which I was trying, unsuccessfully, to locate a lone duckling, the proverbial webbed needle in this fluid haystack.

Finally, there he was, bobbing around despondently amid gentle ripples of water, which, rather worryingly, looked as though even they might overpower him. Through my binoculars I could see the tangle of fishing line that bound him. I couldn't

see the extent of damage done, but, judging by the amount of line visible, things weren't looking good.

Handing the binoculars over to Chris, who'd come to assist me with the rescue, I began to haul Wildlife Aid's trusty rowing boat to the edge of the water.

The result of my rowing escapade was predictable: rescue attempts, 17; ducklings captured, 0. Every time I was within reach of the little fellow, despite his malady, his inherent agility far outswam that of the progress made by my tired arms as I defiantly paddled on. I was, however, close enough on more than one occasion to assess better the duckling's injuries and, consequently, having seen that the wire had begun to cut into the youngster's flesh, knew that I must take a new tack to ensure his imminent treatment.

Following a complex series of arm gestures from me, Chris had begun to prepare the centre's outboard motor from his station on the bank as I wearily approached. Leaving him to get the boat ready, I made my way around the fishermen – who were permitted to fish on the lake by the local angling club – to inform them of my plan. While most were very compassionate upon hearing the young duckling's plight, immediately winding in their lines so as not to hamper either my progress or their equipment, others were less than accommodating. But, neither willing nor able to spare precious moments procrastinating with those less helpful, I wasted no time in returning to my newly empowered vessel.

On the water once more – my two arms spared by a five-horsepower engine, and in response to Chris's binocular-aided navigational gestures – I was back within the struggling duckling's vicinity in no time. Poised above where I'd last seen the youngster dive, I waited, hardly daring to blink for fear of missing his re-emergence from the murky depths. As his young beak broke the water's surface, I swooped down with my net, catching him up in the process. Gently easing him from the net, I was, for the first time, able to get a good look at his entangled predicament. So enmeshed was he in the cruel discarded wire that I knew I wouldn't be able to free him without the surgical precision available to me back at the hospital. Worse still, the line's hook remained attached to the line, and was now embedded in the tiny duckling's neck.

Firing up the outboard motor for our final voyage, I began to steer the boat towards the land. Just a matter of moments into our journey – lo and behold! – the propeller suddenly became jammed with yet more of the cursed fishing line.

Having stopped the engine, I leaned over to cut the wires that were adding dangerous minutes to my getting the young duckling back to the hospital for the treatment he so desperately needed. From my position – some 18 metres out from the shore – I felt quite safe in the choice replies I threw back at one particular angrily protesting bank-bound fisherman.

Although, during the course of this formidable exchange, I couldn't help but wonder why Chris was throwing himself around like a lunatic, I soon found out.

Once back on ground that was becoming less and less solid by the second as Chris recited a disturbing account of his recent findings, I found another reason to prioritise my immediate return to the safety of Wildlife Aid: the angry fisherman (whose severed line was currently still half amalgamated with my semi-immobilised propeller) had only just been released from prison for GBH – more specifically, expressing his whimsical dislike for a person by pouring petrol over him and setting him alight.

Trepidation bubbled in my veins as he approached us. A far cry from the assured (self-proclaimed) heroic wildlife rescuer of only minutes before, I plunged my hand into my pocket and produced a waterlogged ten-pound note. 'Your fishing line … sorry … new one… sorry for… sorry… um, sir,' I stammered, offering him the soggy dilapidated likeness of Her Majesty, and certain that I felt my hand rise a good twenty degrees in temperature as he reached out to snatch it with a reticent grunt.

Having arrived back at the centre in record time, I passed the carry case containing 'Blaze' the duckling to Sara while I went to splash some nice cool water on my face.

Once the hook was removed from his little neck, and its resulting wound stitched, Blaze was cleaned up and doused in Anitrobe (an antibiotic powder) where the (now removed) fishing line had cut in. Intrasite gel was applied to his torn tissue to help it to heal, and for the next week he was given painkillers and antibiotics.

Within a couple of days, Blaze was adopted by the centre's already established group of fellow orphan ducklings. His injuries healed well and, months later, having grown a sleek adult plumage, he was released with his new family back into fisherman-free waters.

MALLARD DUCK FACT FILE

Name	Mallard duck (*Anas platyrynchos*)
Class	Aves
Order	Anseriformes
Family	Anatidae
Terms	Male – drake; female – hen; young – chicks, ducklings; home – nest

Distribution (globally): Mallards can be found almost anywhere in the world, in both the northern and southern hemispheres.

Habitat: They live predominantly in wetlands, where they have easy access to water and food.

Size: They grow to about 50–60cm in length and have a wingspan of up to a metre.

Weight: Between 750g and 1.5kg.

Description: The drake has a black, grey and white body with an easily recognisable dark-green head. Hens are light brown with patches of white and dark brown.

Lifespan
In the wild: 10 – 12 years.
In captivity: Up to 20 years (the oldest duck recorded was 29 years old).

When most commonly seen: Mallards feed throughout the day, so there is no specific time of day to spot them. Mallards, which live in southern countries, remain there all year round. However, those that live in more northern climates will migrate after breeding season to warmer pastures.

Diet: Mallards eat small invertebrates and aquatic vegetation. They filter water through their bills to get vital plant and animal organisms. They will also eat worms and insects when on land.

Reproduction facts: The hens can breed just a year after they are born. Ducks start to pair up sometimes as early as October, but the hens tend to lay their eggs around March. They will lay eggs every few days until they've completed the brood. A brood usually comprises 9–13 eggs and the gestation period lasts about 28 days, while the hen incubates them.

DID YOU KNOW?

After mating, mallards moult into eclipse plumage. This makes them look similar to female ducks.

The mallard is the most abundant waterfowl in the world.

The mallard was first domesticated in Southeast Asia over 2,000 years ago.

In the winter, mallards from Scandinavia and other colder regions come to Britain.

Tuesdays with Robin

The Story of Lucky
the Robin

'Mr Morrie?'

'Oh! Come in, come in.' I was whisked through the ivy-surrounded porch, posthaste, and ushered into a darkened room by an elderly gentleman whose character-lined features were knotted with concern. 'I've kept the little mite in here,' he told me, gesturing towards what had become a very familiar sight to me: a cardboard box covered with a tea towel. 'Warm, dark and quiet, just like you said on the telephone. I peeked in a moment ago, and he was just lying there. I don't think he's breathing.'

Mr Morrie had called me some twenty minutes previously, explaining that he'd returned from his

morning stroll to find the nestling deposited on his doorstep – most likely by way of a gift from next door's moggy. The young robin, he said, had traces of blood on its wing, although he had been unable, at an initial glance, to detect the source.

The fact that there had been a cat involved worried me. A cat's saliva contains many germs that, if they infect even the smallest of puncture wounds, can prove to be a potentially fatal injury to our feathered friends. I had advised my worried caller on how best to keep the bird until I arrived.

Now, leaning over the box, Mr Morrie tentatively peeled back the corner of the encasing tea towel. Without any warning, the bird shot out of the tiny exposed gap in a lightning bid for freedom. Ever the Boy Scout, I reached for the net that I'd brought with me – just in case. Reeling in shock from the robin's miraculous recovery, Mr Morrie instinctively reached for the curtains and, before I could direct him to the contrary, threw open the nearer one, I assumed either to open the window for the bird to pilot itself through, or to let the enabling daylight assist us in its capture. As it transpired, my first guess had been correct. But it was already too late. As Mr Morrie fumbled with the window's lock as quickly as anxious arthritic hands would allow, the bird propelled itself straight past his wispy white hair and crashed painfully against the pane of supposed freedom.

Motionless on the floor below, the bird lay stunned.

Mr Morrie's already crumpled face crumpled further as I lifted the tiny creature's limp form into view. In that instant, a scene from my childhood called to me.

I had been sitting at my parents' kitchen table, a boy of no more than five or six, when a very similar episode had unfolded before me. Hearing a thud on the window at the far side of the room, I had cautiously lowered myself from the rickety old farmhouse bench and hurried towards the glass through which my young eyes were about to witness a miracle.

Having been alerted by the same conspicuous thud, on the other side of the glass, my father had downed his gardening apparatus and was now crouched over a lifeless blue tit. I looked on as he gently picked up the bird and, cupping it in his friendly giant hands, began to breathe into the space between his thumbs, in just such a way as he'd taught me to 'play' blades of grass, using them like a musical instrument's reed, the previous summer. I was transfixed. After a few warm breaths, he moved his hands away from his mouth and slowly began to open out his palms, from which – to my awestruck younger self – soared a healthy bird, high into the air.

Magic, I thought.

My father re-lit his pipe and returned to his vegetable patch.

Enclosing the robin in my own hands, I took a deep breath, and blew gently and steadily between my thumbs. After my third breath, I felt a fluttering sensation against my fingers. Rearranging my grip on the youngster, I removed my left hand to reveal an alert pair of beady black eyes darting this way and that.

This 'avian mouth-to-mouth' technique has proved invaluable to me over the years, providing stunned victims of this particular type of incident with the immediate source of air and warmth necessary to revive them, seemingly miraculously.

'Lucky I called you,' said Mr Morrie.

Back at the centre I examined 'Lucky' for puncture injuries and, finding none, decided that the traces of blood evident on his feathers must have come from the cat as the young robin had clawed its defence. Estimating the little one's age, judging by the fluffy grey tufts of 'hair' on either side of its head, to be two to three weeks, I put the youngster in an incubator with a nest of similarly aged chicks and gave them their two-hourly feed of chopped maggots by way of a pair of plastic yellow tweezers resembling a mother's beak.

Mr Morrie's robin thrived, and nine weeks later, together with his foster brothers and sisters, was released into the fruit cage at Wildlife Aid. Here at the centre, we refer to this as a 'soft release', the interim stage between hospital care and 'the wild'. After a month of perfecting their aerobatics and mastering the art of seeking out food and feeding for themselves, the robins were collected up and released in the (cat-free) garden of one of our volunteers.

EUROPEAN ROBIN FACT FILE

Name European robin (*Erithacus rubecula*)
Class Aves
Order Passeriformes
Family Turdidae

Distribution (globally): They live across Europe, North Africa and some parts of the Middle East.

Habitat: Robins like hedgerows, gardens, parks and woodlands.

Size: They grow to about 15cm in length (from beak to tail), with a wingspan of about 20cm.

Weight: Between 15 and 22g.

Description: Robins have brown backs and wings, with a bright-red breast and face. Underneath this red breast is a greyish patch. Contrary to popular belief, there is no difference in appearance between the male and female. However, young robins have no red feathers at all.

Lifespan: Up to 8 years.

When most commonly seen: All year round.

Diet: Their main source of food is insects, but they also feed on seeds and fruit.

Reproduction facts: The female builds a nest and lays 4–6 eggs. She then incubates them for about 2 weeks before they hatch. The robin can have 3 broods in one year. The young are fully fledged in only a couple of weeks.

DID YOU KNOW?

Robins are so aggressive towards each other that they have been known to attack their own reflection and other red objects.

The robin is Britain's national bird, selected over 40 years ago.

Robins sing all year round, and their alarm call is a 'tick'.

The Good Wife

The Story of Snow White's Barn Owls

'*A*-*choo!*'

'Bless you!' I countered, as I opened the door to the hospital. Slightly confused as to the origin of the sneeze, since neither half of the elderly couple who stood before me looked to be recovering from such an outburst, I allowed my gaze to fall upon the lady's familiar tentative offering of a cardboard box.

'They're Snow White's little ones,' she informed me, proceeding then to introduce her husband, Peter, and herself as Vivienne.

'Simon,' I said, offering my hand.

'Arthur,' she said.

'Simon,' I repeated, louder this time, puzzled as to

the utter lack of phonetic resemblance between the two titles.

'Arthur,' she confirmed, and, noticing the fond look that Peter bestowed upon the top of her untamed white hair, I retreated: 'Arthur.' Shifting his twinkly eyed smile briefly in my direction, Peter acknowledged my acquiescence with a silent nod of gratitude.

After accepting the box from Vivienne, I placed it on the examination table and, on lifting its lid, was met by a collage of fluff and big round ebony eyes. 'A-choo!' wheezed one of the barn owl chicks, fluffing himself up and shaking his head simultaneously. 'That's Sneezy,' said Vivienne, pointing at the chick immediately to the left of the one that had just sneezed. 'Happy, Sleepy and Bashful' (who toppled over right on cue, waking up Sleepy).

In authentic hypnotic storyteller tones, Peter told me how he and Vivienne had married just after the war and moved to the farm just outside Dorking where they had raised their family and remained for the past fifty years. Peter had chosen to keep the farmland as natural as possible, rejecting 'modern ways' in favour of nature's, and thus keeping the land rich in the native wildlife that he loved so much.

Every year, without fail, their barn had served as

shelter to nesting barn owls. The couple had delighted, over the years, in witnessing the comings and goings of dozens of families of the graceful birds of prey. This year, however, proceedings had not commenced as experience dictated they should, with the parent owls conspicuous by their ever-lengthening absence. Days went by, and still there was no sign of activity around the nesting sight. Fearing for the safety of the chicks, Peter had felt he'd no choice but to intervene, removing the youngsters from the nest and bringing them to us.

Later that evening, as I fed the gawky youngsters – at this early age so utterly unrecognisable as the sleek, streamlined birds of prey that they were to grow into – their two-hourly meal of chopped-up chick, Sara came to me with the news that Peter had called the centre to say there'd been a sighting of an adult barn owl just outside the barn. Wasting no time, I prepared the chicks for a journey and, accompanied by the *Wildlife SOS* camera crew, embarked on the short drive to Dorking.

Peter and Vivienne's farm was exactly as I had pictured it. Bathed in the sleepy golden rays of a summer evening's sun, it was a scene unmistakably reminiscent of the setting for one of Beatrix Potter's tales.

Peter – complete with flat cap and pipe – and Vivienne were waiting for us in the dusty driveway, like an ageing Tom and Barbara from *The Good Life*, ready to escort us to the barn.

I was just about to make the necessary introductions when, 'Simon,' cooed Vivienne from under her lashes (to Jim), 'we've so enjoyed watching you on the television. You've such a way with the animals. Please, call me Viv.' Having been warned, and thus unsurprised, Jim accepted the misdirected compliment graciously. A little thrown, I continued, 'And this is Jo, our soundman, Viv.'

'Hello, John! And it's *Vivienne*, Arthur,' she corrected me with a measured smile.

The barn befitted its rustic situation perfectly, piled high with bales of hay, shards of gentle light reflecting each sweet-smelling fleck of summer dust in their path. After leading me over to a rickety old ladder towards the back of the barn, Peter pointed out to me the carefully carpentered nesting box that had housed the youngsters.

Feeling I needed more proof that the owl seen out in the yard earlier that day was definitely parent to the youngsters, I ascended the ladder in search of clues, a fresh kill in the nesting box, or, indeed, any sign at all of recent activity therein. Craning my neck to see into the box, I witnessed proof indeed, in the form of a further two healthy young chicks. Peter obviously hadn't seen them camouflaged within the nest of feathers and twigs. Given that the chicks seemed nourished and preened, I was in no doubt at all that they were being looked after, and that at least one of the parent owls was still very much 'on the scene'.

As I transferred my four owlets from carry case to nesting box, their two siblings, by now accustomed to the extra space, clucked and clicked their beaks disapprovingly as they shuffled and bunched up to accommodate the return of their brothers and sisters. It was hard to tell which of the two remaining owlets was Grumpy, I thought, as they glowered at me, and each other, alternately.

Attaching a tiny night-vision camera to the outside of the box as quickly as I could, I made my way back down the ladder with its joining cable. I ran the cable all the way outside and through the yard, to a tent that Jim and Jo had pitched some 15 metres away from the barn to accommodate a monitor and the three of us.

We favoured this method of observation for safety reasons – both the youngsters' and our own. The parent owl was unlikely to return to her babies if she sensed our presence, on top of which cameraman Jim had concerns of his own, knowing a fellow cameraman to have lost an eye to a barn owl. An adult barn owl will attack unprovoked, its silent flight making it all the more dangerous for unwitting prey of any species.

With the night drawing in, we waited in hope. *Approximately two hours later, on the screen of our monitor, we witnessed Snow White's reunion with her young. Fresh from an evening's hunt, she'd returned with a tasty morsel, which, after tearing up, she fed to each youngster in turn.*

BARN OWL FACT FILE

Name	Barn owl (*Tyto alba*)
Class	Aves
Order	Strigiformes
Family	Tytonidae

Distribution (globally): Barn owls are distributed extensively across the globe, including most of Europe, Southern Asia, Africa and parts of America and Australia. The barn owl is one of the most widespread species of bird in the world.

Habitat: Barn owls like to nest within natural holes in trees, old buildings and barns. They inhabit large uncultivated areas such as marshes, heaths and forests. They are also found on farmland and in some gardens.

Size: Barn owls grow to around 35–40cm tall; they have a wingspan of 80–95cm.

Weight: Females weigh slightly more than males. Males average at about 300g, while females tend to be between 300 and 375g.

Description: They have golden upper parts and white underparts. Barn owls have a white heart-shaped face, with large black eyes.

Lifespan
In the wild: Between 10 and 15 years.
In captivity: Maximum of 21 years.

When most commonly seen: Barn owls are typically nocturnal, but can be seen during the day when feeding their young.

Diet: They mainly feed on small mammals, such as mice and voles. However, they do sometimes hunt other smaller birds.

Reproduction facts: Barn owls tend to pair up for life, so they typically live alone or in pairs. Females lay their eggs between April and May; a usual clutch consists of 4–7 eggs. They are laid at intervals and hatch after 33 days. Although the eggs are incubated solely by the female, the male does help to feed the chicks. Young barn owls remain in the nest for a long period of time, usually 9–12 weeks.

DID YOU KNOW?

Owl broth used to be given as a treatment for coughs in the north. People likened the sound of a cough to the 'whooping' sounds of the bird, and believed that, for this reason, it would cure their cough.

There are 30 subspecies of the barn owl, ranging across most of the world.

The short feathers that form a barn owl's face enhance the bird's hearing by forming a groove that helps to direct sound waves to the ear opening.

Barn owls do not hoot: they make long shrieking noises.

Rabbit from a Trap

The Story of Bun
the Rabbit

I wound up the car window, turned the heating dial to full and willed the windscreen wipers on as they grittily battled the cruel weather. It was unseasonably cold for the time of year. The formerly clear, spring-promising skies had bruised over the course of the past week and, now moody and defensive, seemed intent on covering nature's tentative awakenings with a thick, suffocating blanket of snow.

Arriving at my destination, I transferred the numbers scrawled on the Post-it note stuck to my steering wheel to the keypad of my mobile phone.

'Lucy? I'm here – I think,' I said.

'Simon. I see you,' replied the worried female

voice. 'We're just nearing the car park now. I'll come and fetch you.'

In an attempt to stay warm, I busied myself with assembling a small pile of the equipment that I would need, placing next to the car a pair of gloves and some sturdy wire cutters on top of a carry case containing a thick towel. As I reached up to close the boot, I glimpsed two colourful figures approaching through the misty glass. Walking round the side of the car, I was met by a woman and her tearful young daughter ('I'm Izzie and I'm seven and three-quarters,' I was quickly informed through whole-body-encompassing shudders), both clad in a mishmash of bulky winter clothing.

Trudging through the snow, I learned that the pair had been out walking their dog ('Sid – he's three and one half'), when the little Westie had begun digging excitedly at the snow, sniffing a patch of recently uncovered earth and wagging his tail furiously. Calling Sid back ('Mummy thought he was eating poo again'), Lucy had discovered a small rabbit tangled in wire, which she had thought to be some kind of trap. The wires had begun to cut into the frightened youngster and, worried that she might inflict further injury by trying to free it, she had contacted the local police ('Why don't *you* have blue flashing nee nah nee nah lights?'), who had, in turn, referred her to us.

Once she was back at the scene, the temporarily brightened spirits of young Izzie ('short for 'lizabeff') crumbled once more, bringing forth a fresh torrent of tears. I bent down over the fragile wounded creature, which was lying abandoned in a tangle of wire that I immediately identified as a 'free-running snare'.

Although legal, provided they are set and positioned correctly, these snares can cause horrific injuries and often a very slow, painful death. The free-running snare works like a slipknot, by way of a loop of wire that traps the animal, tightening as the creature tries to free itself. They are set by farmers or gamekeepers to stop rabbits from eating young shoots and decimating crops.

There are several types of trap, the most vicious of which being the gin trap – a powerfully sprung, jawed clamp of serrated metal teeth triggered by a footplate, which, thankfully, was made illegal back in the 1940s. However, there are still legal traps available, such as Fenn traps, which, by way of a spring-loaded clamp, are designed to kill the animal outright by breaking its neck like an oversized mouse trap.

Handling the young rabbit as gently as I could, I parted its fur where the wire had fastened itself, and was relieved to see that, for all the little one's obvious initial struggles for freedom, the wire had not cut too deeply into its flesh.

In our dealings with wild animals, our main enemy is stress. These frightened creatures don't understand that, often, the hands that hurt them are then trying to help them – how could they? So, though I knew that the injuries to this particular youngster were not, in themselves, life-threatening, in combination with stress they could well be fatal. Time was, as always, of the essence.

'Is he g-g-going t-to h-h-heaven?' asked a small shuddering voice to my side.

Exchanging a measured glance with the little girl's mother, I said, with more confidence than I felt, 'Not just yet.'

With Lucy cradling the young rabbit in her blue-mittened hands, I managed to cut it free of the wire. I quickly put my thumbnail to the youngster's back foot, tweaking the pad of its toe lightly, in response to which the rabbit instinctively jerked its foot away, indicating to me that there was no spinal damage done. Not wanting to prolong the youngster's exposure to the cold any longer, I wrapped him up in a towel and cushioned him in the carry case.

The walk back to the car was a sombre one. In a regrettable attempt to lighten the mood, I had proffered some humour.

'Izzie?'

'Mm?' She looked up at me with sad, wide eyes.

91

I smiled. 'What do you get if you pour boiling water down a rabbit hole?'

With an incredulous expression that rested somewhere between anger and sheer horror at my apparent gross insensitivity, she stated thunderously, 'A dead rabbit!'

'No, no, it's a jo— I was just trying to –' I fumbled, but she wasn't listening.

'And they're not called *holes*: they're called *warrens*,' she said firmly.

'Yes, indeed they are. I... um... A hot cross bun,' I concluded lamely.

Back at the centre, with Sara's help, I applied Anitrobe to the young rabbit's wounds, along with Intrasite – a gel that would help his wounds to heal. 'Bun' was given oral Baytril (another antibiotic) and some painkillers every day for a week, over the course of which his wounds began to granulate. At around five weeks old, the youngster was just about old enough to be feeding for himself, so a collection of 'roots and shoots' from the grounds of the centre was left in his cage, in addition to some vegetables and grass, and a bowl of milk substitute.

A cool, calm, healed Bun was released into the field backing on to the centre two weeks later.

RABBIT FACT FILE

Name	European rabbit (Oryctolagus cuniculus)
Class	Mammal
Order	Lagomorpha
Family	Mustelidae
Terms	Male – buck; female – doe; young – kitten; home – warren

Distribution (globally): The European rabbit can be found around Europe, North Africa, Australasia, North and South America.

Habitat: Rabbits can be found anywhere that they can burrow, from open meadows to heath land to sand dunes. However, they try to avoid damp conditions and coniferous woodlands.

Size: Rabbits usually grow to about 30–45cm in length from head to tail.

Weight: 1.2–2.2kg.

Description (looks): Rabbits' bodies are brown/grey, they have long ears with brown tips, and long hind legs. They have short fluffy tails which are brown on the top and white underneath.

Lifespan
In the wild: Up to 9 years.
In captivity: 7–10 years, maximum of 15.

When most commonly seen: All year round. They tend to be active during the evening and night. However, if they live in an area undisturbed by man, they can be seen during the day.

Diet: Rabbits eat a variety of vegetation, leaves, grass and bulbs. They also eat their own faeces to maximise its nutritional value.

Reproduction facts: Rabbits can breed at any time of year, but the main season is from January to August. Females can actually have one litter a month during this period. The usual size of a litter is between 3 and 7 babies; it can, however, be as large as 12. A typical gestation period lasts about 31 days and the young are weaned after 28 days.

DID YOU KNOW?

Rabbits were introduced to Britain in the twelfth century to provide meat and fur.

Tunnelling in the warren is taken up predominantly by the females.

Competition between female rabbits for nest sites often leads to serious injury, even death.

Rabbits thump their hind legs and raise their tails to show the white part as a warning signal.

Chim Chim-in-ey

The Story of Sooty, Sweep, Sue and Bob, the Jackdaws

I decided to cover all possible bases as I loaded the car. My understanding of the situation was thus: a Mrs Waterman, being in the final throes of having her house renovated from top to bottom, had employed the services of a chimney sweep and, upon venturing out with a tray containing a piping-hot cup of tea and Waitrose's finest assortment of chocolate biscuits (she had found the work of her various employees over the last year to have improved notably at the introduction of just such an elevenses sweetening), the lady of the house had discovered her latest tradesman craning over the ageing chimney, wearing – underneath a thick layer of black-sooted foundation – a somewhat baffled expression.

Daintily – much to Mrs Waterman's quiet amusement – sipping his tea from one of her bone-china mugs five minutes later and two storeys lower, the towering sweep explained that he'd come across a nest of gaping orange beaks lodged halfway down the chimney flume and, unable to reach them from either direction, was at a bit of a loss as to what to do for fear of hurting the youngsters. Hearing this, a concerned Mrs Waterman had immediately recalled her previous Sunday afternoon's viewing, *Wildlife SOS*, whereupon she set about an investigation regarding the programme's origin. Tracking down Wildlife Aid, she called to see if we could be of assistance.

Having recruited Chris – one of the centre's younger volunteers (and possibly more open to the idea of scaling roofs) – I punched in the Sussex address to my GPS, and we were off.

Half an hour later, I found myself a good 9 or 10 metres higher than I was strictly comfortable with, looking down at Chris as he watched the screen intently, shouting out directions to me. The best course of action, I had decided after weighing up the entirety of the youngsters' predicament, was to go back to basics. I wasn't unduly worried about the chicks: they were gaping for food and, with evidently healthy lungs, calling for their mum. Due to the fact that the nest was indeed located at an unreachable juncture, I had formulated a plan.

Borrowing a soup ladle and a coat hanger from an understandably perplexed Mrs Waterman, and two of the amenable chimney sweeps' brushes, I strapped the ladle firmly to the handle end of one of the brushes and, after a bit of metal manipulation, the coat hanger to the other, along with a tiny video camera – the signal from which was being received by Chris on a portable monitor below.

Using the coat-hangered brush, and guided by Chris, I gently scooped one chick at a time into the ladle, which I then fed up as carefully as I could to the waiting hands of my eager chimney-sweep accomplice. As gently as if he were handling a newborn child, he cradled each nestling between ladle and carry case. Once the last chick was safely retrieved, I poked the nest free of its sooty hollow and into the waiting fireplace below.

Being, by a wide margin, the less ladder-friendly of the two of us, I entrusted the carry case of chattering young jackdaws to the sweep. The birds were lowered by his safe hand with a considered, stealthy precision. Such adjectives could not be used to depict my own wobbly descent.

Once we were grounded, Mrs Waterman led me into her home to recover the babies' crumbled former abode. I collected up the various pieces of twig and moss, deciding that I would later use them to line the youngsters' incubator back at the centre – hopefully giving them a sense of familiarity.

Chris and I bade our farewells to Mrs Waterman and her friendly chimney sweep, the combination of whom, standing waving into our rear-view mirror, strangely resembled a scene from *Mary Poppins*.

Back at the centre, to a soundtrack of the youngsters' hungrily cried 'tchack!' noises, I raced to chop maggots and spoon out cat food. Finally, administering a dose of Sara's 'secret-recipe' vitamin mixture, the chicks' mushed-up gourmet meal was ready for their impatient consumption. I tweezered an equal portion into each gaping yellow beak in turn, until the content and exhausted little ones settled, with satisfied stomachs, into a much-deserved slumber.

The growing jackdaws would need two-hourly feeds throughout the days of the six weeks that followed, but not so during the night, since this wouldn't be the practice of their parents in the wild. An additional month in the second hospital – the halfway house of their adolescence – and the young birds would be ready for the last leg of their stay at Wildlife Aid: flight school in an outdoor aviary.

The Jackdaw family flourished at the centre. Jackdaws are a resilient species, not as prone to shock as some of the centre's other youngsters. Sooty, Sweep, Sue and

Bob (the last name was for lack of a fourth character within the popular TV classic that had seemed such an apt naming device initially!) provided the staff of Wildlife Aid with hours of entertainment in their time at the centre, their raucous voices seeing fit to comment at ear-splitting volume on anything from new arrivals to offered cups of tea!

The sleek young adult birds were released back into Mrs Waterman's garden and are frequently seen convening on the mesh above the chimney.

JACKDAW FACT FILE

Name	Jackdaw (*Corvus monedula*)
Class	Aves
Order	Passeriformes
Family	Corvidae

Distribution (globally): Jackdaws are found in most areas of Britain and Europe. They can also be seen in parts of Asia and North Africa.

Habitat: Jackdaws live in a variety of habitats, ranging from woods to grasslands to sea cliffs. In towns, they will live in roofs and chimneys.

Size: Usually about 32–34cm in length, with a wingspan of 70–90cm.

Weight: 180–260g.

Description: The jackdaw is the smallest of Britain's crows. They are mainly black in colour, with grey necks and underparts.

Lifespan: About 14 years.

When most commonly seen: All year round.

Diet: Jackdaws eat many different types of food, depending on what they can get. Their main food source is worms, insects and seeds. However, they do raid other birds' nests for eggs and nestlings. They also love insect larvae and will peck at bark to get these.

Reproduction facts: Jackdaws reach sexual maturity after one year; the mating period is between April and June. A typical brood consists of 4–5 eggs, which are incubated for about 18 days. The young are usually fledged after about 32 days.

DID YOU KNOW?

Jackdaws sometimes dip their food into water before eating it.

It used to be believed that slitting a jackdaw's tongue would make it a good mimic of the human voice.

Jackdaws land on sheep's backs to collect wool for their nests.

Gentle Giant

The Story of Li'l,
the Little Owl

I gulped. It was all I could think to do, to be honest. Before me towered a giant, blocking out what had formerly been a rather spectacular view of the full moon and, indeed, most of the stars.

I had been in my kitchen, shutting up shop for the night and awaiting my dogs' return from their evening constitutional, when I had spotted a figure in the driveway. Curious (if not a little apprehensive, as the stranger's stature seemed to grow in metres at a time, rather than inches, as he loomed ever closer), I'd stood my ground in the doorway.

Clad from head to toe in leather – as imposing as it was beat up – stood all of my childhood nightmares personified. With my entire life flashing

before my very eyes, I silently prayed that my imminent demise would be quick and painless, that someone would remember to give my ageing golden retriever, Sam, his Rimadyl tablet each night in my absence, and that this colossal (supposed) human being was not in fact the new beau of either one of my beautiful daughters.

As the giant raised its arm (and I held my breath), nothing could have prepared me for what came next. Pushing aside a mop of dishevelled hair from his face, a much unexpected picture was revealed. The giant was crying.

Bemusedly, I followed his mottled gaze and was incredulous to see, as he pulled back one side of his jacket, a tiny little owl nestled carefully in its inside pocket. With tears now streaming freely down his ruddy, bearded cheeks, and thus looking infinitely less intimidating, he said, 'Li'l soul jus' flew strigh' in a' me win'screen. There were nuthin' I cu' do!' I pushed the front door further open behind me, indicating for him to follow me into the house and noticing as I did so the beginnings of what I was later to learn was a 17-tonne lorry strewn across my driveway (and the majority of the road).

Using one of the surfaces in my utility room as a makeshift examination table, I laid the little owl down. To be flying, the youngster had to be around twelve weeks old, probably out on one of her maiden voyages, I suspected, not used to the dangers of cars and still not quite in command of the necessary coordination to avoid such hazardous situations.

As I gently assessed the patient, I began to piece together – between the heavy shuddering breaths of its rescuer – the story of just how this little owl had come to be in the inside pocket of a leather jacket.

The giant was in fact a lorry driver named Tom. Tom had been nearing the end of his night's work, just pulling off the motorway, when out of nowhere the owl had tumbled from the sky and collided with his windscreen. He'd pulled his huge lorry to the side of the road. This was no mean feat, I was assured with the aid of a flurry of animated arm gestures that, without looking round, I was quite sure were not in accordance with the various ornaments and possessions of mine positioned anywhere within the vicinity of his 10–foot arm span. He'd then hurried back out into the traffic and scooped up the 'li'l ol'' before any further harm could come to it. 'I didn' know wha' t'do!' he told me with glassy eyes as wide as saucers.

As it transpired, he'd spent half an hour calling round his friends, until one had suggested us, having seen an article about Wildlife Aid in his local paper. Tom had driven for over an hour and a half to our door, only to find the hospital closed up for the night, open solely for emergency callouts. Undeterred, and for the sake of his feathered friend in need, he'd made his way towards the light of my kitchen.

I was very concerned for the little owl, who, upon my initial examination, seemed to be in a considerable degree of shock. Her half-closed eyes were not the alert, round, piercing yellow that I would expect from such a bird, and, dazed, she seemed unable to stand, preferring instead to lie on her side. Her left wing, although drooping badly, on closer inspection appeared to be undamaged (a fact that was later confirmed by an X-ray). It was just bruised, I surmised. One of the first tests I usually carry out on a bird of prey involves placing my finger against its talons. It's like a doctor's knee-jerk reflex test: a healthy bird will grip tightly, curling each talon around the offered finger. This little one's talons remained relaxed.

I explained to Tom that I was going to keep his 'li'l ol'' in a warm, dark box overnight – the temperature would need to be in the region of 80°F (about 27°C) to combat the bird's shock – and that, for the same reason, it was imperative that the young owl be kept totally away from human contact. To her we were objects of fear, looming over her like dinosaurs over an ant. Tom understood and bade her a gentle farewell, to which she 'clucked' almost imperceptibly, but to Tom it was more than enough.

The next morning, I was delighted to find Li'l Ol' (Li'l for short) a very much brighter bird indeed. Pulled up to her full height – of 5 inches – she bobbed around in front of me comically, her clear amber eyes following my every movement as I chopped up the dead day-old chick that was to be her breakfast. Gently holding open her beak, I tweezered a few small portions of chick into her mouth which she gulped down appreciatively. Leaving the rest of the meal in a shallow bowl towards the front of her cage, I left her to her own devices, hoping she would be tempted to feed for herself.

Two hours later I was standing in front of an empty bowl and a full little owl. Li'l was looking every bit the sleek bird of prey that she would eventually be, just as soon as the giveaway tufty fluff of owlet-hood had dispersed.

I chuckled, watching Li'l, as I remembered Tom's exuberant thanks (and winced as my back did the same, recalling the clap it had received at the grateful hand of the giant – repeatedly). After taking down the number for the centre, so he could call to check on her progress the following morning, Tom had turned to leave. One defiant 'crack' (his head meeting the top of the door frame) – to which, other than a slight stumble, he seemed entirely oblivious – and he was gone.

Li'l stayed at Wildlife Aid until she was fully fledged; she was then released not far from the centre into a known parliament of little owls.

LITTLE OWL FACT FILE

Name Little owl (*Athene noctua*)
Class Aves
Order Strigiformes
Family Tytonidae

Distribution (globally): Little owls live all over Europe and in some parts of North Africa, Asia and the Middle East.

Habitat: Because little owls are so widely spread around the globe, they live in a variety of places. Little owls can be found anywhere, from deserts to mountain ranges to countryside forests. In Britain, they are found to nest mostly in hedgerows.

Size: Usually 19–25cm tall, with a wingspan of up to 60cm.

Weight: 100–200g.

Description: The little owl is the smallest owl to be found in Britain. They have a predominantly white belly with grey and brown patches. The rest of their bodies are covered in mainly brown and grey plumage with the odd white spot. They have bright-yellow eyes and possess an unmistakable 'frowning' face.

Lifespan
In the wild: 3 years (highest recorded 10 years).

In captivity: 10 years.

When most commonly seen: Little owls are crepuscular (active at dusk and dawn) but sometimes hunt during the day. They are present all year round.

Diet: They eat insects, worms and small mammals, such as mice. Little owls also eat small rabbits and fish and are one of the only owls known to eat vegetation.

Reproduction facts: Female little owls breed

after one year; they lay their eggs between April and May. A typical female will lay 3–5 eggs, which take about 29 days to hatch. The young owls fledge in, typically, 26–35 days.

DID YOU KNOW?

Little owls were not introduced to Britain until about a hundred years ago.

At first, it is only the male owl who feeds the newborn chicks.

The owl is the emblem of the Greek goddess Athene, which is why it takes the scientific binomial *Athene noctua* (genus and species).

Orphan Alfie

The Story of Alfie
the Fox Cub

The call had been made by a police officer at around three in the morning. He and his partner had found a recently killed female fox in the road and, although they could find neither hide nor hair of it now, they had seen a young cub at her side, gently nuzzling her face as though silently pleading with her to wake up. Pulling their car over to get a better look had scared the youngster, and it had fled into the undergrowth.

I had asked that they have a closer look at the mother fox's body – explaining what her teats would look like had she indeed been lactating (breastfeeding cubs). The policeman confirmed that the vixen's teats were quite swollen, and so, anxious that the newly

orphaned cub should not perish, I had assembled the necessary equipment: a pair of thick gloves, a carrying cage and a grasper. This is a long-handled pole with a lasso-type end, the pressure of which can be increased or decreased as necessary; such a provision, in this instance, might not be necessary, but I was unsure how old the cub would be.

Upon arriving at the scene, I carefully parked my car behind the dead vixen's body so as to protect any cubs that might run out into oncoming traffic. I then sat stock still on the roadside, straining to hear the telltale signs of rustling or quiet 'mewing' within the surrounding hedgerows, all the while shining a torch out into the darkness. This, I had discovered some time ago, was the best way to locate an animal in the wee small hours – its eyes reflecting the light from the beam, as cat's eyes do on a road at night.

Hearing the dark stir somewhere off to my left, I made my way quietly down the muddy bank at the side of the road, only to find the frightened cub shivering behind a large rock. Instantly I could tell that the cub must be approximately three weeks old, for, although its eyes were open, its coat was still a rich chocolate-brown colour – a detail that often leads people to assume that they are looking at a domestic kitten. Knowing that a cub of this tender age posed me no threat, I quietly knelt down and scooped it up. Having wrapped him in a towel for warmth, I placed the youngster in the carrying cage, which I put down beside me, hoping that the little creature's cries would attract any of its brothers and sisters who may or may not be lurking nearby.

An hour later, there was still no sign of any more youngsters. Worried that the cub would be getting cold and hungry, I made the difficult decision to set off back to the centre.

Once we were inside the warmth of the hospital, I was thinking about how people are often too quick to interfere with nature's ways as a pair of azure–blue oceans gazed up at me, partly obscured by the teat of a baby's bottle. Tragically, in this particular instance, human intervention had been unavoidable if this youngster was to survive, but, in general, animals will habitually leave their young for periods of time that seem like an age to us. The danger with human interference is that, once a youngster is handled, and therefore bathed in human scent, the mother will not accept it back into the fold.

I remembered an incident from the previous year when our team was called out to deal with a litter of cubs that had been found under a garden shed that was being renovated. The member of the public who'd called us had, luckily, not touched the cubs at all. As soon as we arrived at the scene, wearing thick gloves, which we had first rubbed diligently in soil and grass to disguise our scent, we transferred the cubs to a secure area – a makeshift 'earth' that they couldn't get out of, but their mother, if she was still in the vicinity, could get into. Having placed the babies into their temporary sanctuary, we set up CCTV and camped out in the car for the night, watching the activities of the cubs from a monitor plugged into the cigarette lighter of our trusty silver Volvo.

In the early hours of the morning, to my utter amazement, a vixen skulked up to our temporary enclosure. Hardly daring to hope, I held my breath in anticipation. She circled the litter of whimpering cubs, and stole away once more into the darkness. I exhaled sheer disappointment. But half an hour later she was back. This time, she leaned into the den, gently picked up one of the cubs by the scruff of its neck and trotted off once more whence she came. Breath stolen, I waited. She made the same journey a further five times, even returning for a sixth visit to check that she had safely transferred her entire family.

I was incredulous.

On this occasion, once it was fed and content, I placed the young cub into an incubator with a teddy bear to snuggle up to for company in lieu of the comfort of its mother – a sorry substitute if ever there was one, but better than nothing for the bewildered little orphan, I decided.

First thing the following morning, I was off back to the scene of the previous night's rescue to see if I could find any sign of the rest of the litter, and to ask any neighbours if they had seen anything of the youngsters I suspected might return.

Alfie's siblings never returned to the site of their mother's demise, so, in time, Alfie was placed with a group of the centre's similarly aged orphaned fox cubs. At about three and a half months old, Alfie and his new family were ready for Wildlife Aid's Soft Release Programme.

Finding a local landowner happy to have them (and not located in a built-up area), our volunteers arrived at the designated nearby farm to build a soft-release pen. We have four or five such pens at the centre that we can assemble and dismantle easily – they are six-sided (including top and bottom) and have a double door so that we can go in without fear that the pens' occupants might escape. These pens, which we're always sure to install well away from people or dogs, have within them sleeping boxes, branches and general foliage for the young animals to play with. Once an animal is released into the soft-release pen, the relevant person provides food and water for anywhere between two and three weeks – depending on how quickly the youngsters go wild, at which point the animals are allowed to 'escape'. The doors to the pen are left open, and food put out within it for as long as the young foxes are still returning to take it, until such time as they naturally disperse. The soft-release pen is then dismantled and taken back to the centre in preparation for the next litter.

Out-foxed

The Story of Annette
the Fox Cub

At last. A clear, blue sky. Though infinitely more appealing through the secured warmth of my office's double glazing than I knew its winter-exuding temperatures to be in actuality, it was, nonetheless, a welcome sight. I was not alone in my view, it would seem.

The rest of the world, also apparently buoyed by the welcome sight of spring's open arms, had decided, in preparation for a season of typical British sun–worshipping, to address the small matter of their overgrown gardens accordingly.

The centre's switchboard had gone into near meltdown with the volume of calls received during this one morning alone and, having seen more than

twenty springs bloom from the vantage point of Wildlife Aid's head office, I knew that it wouldn't be cooling down any time soon.

The coinciding of the fairer weather's onset with the birth of our native wildlife's offspring is inevitable. The unfortunate side effect to the nation's outdoor spring clean, however, is the inadvertent disruption to our wildlife's homes as they prepare to raise new families of their own.

Shifting my gaze from blue to red – sky to frantically lit switchboard – I hit the nearest key. 'Hello. Wildlife Aid.'

Half an hour later, I was to be found on hands and knees, grappling with handfuls of netting and fox cub.

It was a story regrettably similar to those that had flooded through Wildlife Aid's call centre so many times before. The year's infant sun had prompted the Williams family to renovate their potting shed of all things. Ripping up the well-trodden floorboards of Mr Williams' former garden retreat, though, had unearthed a litter of young foxes. In the general confusion, before anyone knew what was happening, the four young cubs had shot out in the directions of the four main points of the compass.

A quartet of whirling dervishes, the cubs had torn about the small garden, quickly finding an escape route in the form of a small hole in the surrounding chain-meshed fence. One after another, the first three cubs had scurried through the tiny gap, but the fourth, panicky at being left behind, had opted for a nearby smaller hole. This second opening, being slightly higher off the ground than the first, had required the scared youngster to take its opportunity of escape at a running jump. A combination of the force vested in such a leap and the negligible size of the break in the mesh had the result that the cub had got herself stuck, dangling from the fence about a metre from the ground, literally hanging herself. Thrashing wildly in a desperate bid for freedom, she was only becoming more and more entangled by the second.

Horrified at the sight of the frenzied youngster, Mrs Williams had rushed into the house to call the Wildlife Aid helpline.

Knowing full well that a cub of the size that was described to me over the phone was more than capable of inflicting a nasty nip, I'd come prepared with thick gloves, grasper and head vet nurse Sara. In cases such as these, it isn't simply a matter of cutting the necessary binds to release the trapped animal, as no wild creature will sit still awaiting its rescue under such a circumstance. Often it is in its own struggle to free itself that it sustains its worst injuries, thus requiring a thorough examination and, more often than not, treatment at a centre such as Wildlife Aid. To cut the youngster free *and* keep it from running away would require at least four hands. Luckily, between us, Sara and I were ably equipped!

It is possible to still most wild animals by 'scruffing' them – gripping them securely by the loose skin around the back of their neck – as this is the hold that their parents would use to move them around in the wild, and so is familiar to them. As it was, though, this young fox's scruff was inaccessible, obscured by the netting that ensnared her.

So, with Sara posted on one side of the fence, hands covered in thick gloves, holding the cub's body as steady as she could, I ran around the outside of the property to see what I could do. Even with my own gloves on, trying to cut the youngster free as it growled and frequently whipped its head back at lightning speed – puppy-esque needle-sharp teeth at the ready – was a hair-raising experience. Seizing the moments when and wherever I could, I used wire cutters to sever the strands of netting that were holding the cub – all of which were located far too close to her snapping jaw for comfort.

Having freed the youngster from the majority of the knotted twine, I checked with Sara that she had a good grip before cutting the final few strands. Grasping the scruff of the cub the instant that her freedom had been restored, I was able to lift her from the fence and survey the extent of the wounds to her neck.

Sara and I quickly decided that, sadly, releasing the youngster straight back into the wild wasn't an option. Her wounds would leave her wide open to infection, and, besides, her siblings – together with their mother – were by now long gone.

Back at Wildlife Aid, Sara began by cleaning the cub's injured neck with iodine and water, removing any dead tissue with tweezers and, as gently as she could, scrubbing out the wound. Due to contamination, the cuts couldn't be sutured. Instead, each was covered with Intrasite and the cub was put on a course of antibiotics and painkillers. This procedure of cleaning and Intrasite would need to be repeated daily until the wounds granulated.

Once the cub's skin had healed over, she was, being the first cub of the season, introduced to Wildlife Aid's first badger cub of the year. This may seem like an odd pairing, but it is one that we have found to work tremendously well over the years. The two cubs – too young to understand that they are a different species – play well together, providing each other with the stimulus needed by youngsters to help them develop, and a far preferable alternative to either human intervention or a stuffed toy that would otherwise suffice to serve as 'a comforter' to each orphan.

Annette, as we called her, eventually joined an orphaned family of fox-cub youngsters that arrived at the centre the following week. She bonded well with them, and together they spent the rest of their time at the centre before, months later, returning to the wild by virtue of our Soft Release Programme.

FOX FACT FILE

Name Red fox (*Vulpes vulpes*)
Class Mammal
Order Carnivora
Family Canidae
Terms Male – dog; female – vixen; young –
cub; home – den or earth
(for breeding)

Distribution (globally): The red fox can be found across the UK, Europe, North Africa, North America and even some parts of Asia.

Habitat: A huge range, from sand dunes to cities to mountain tops.

Size: The average size of a male fox's body is

67–72cm long, a female roughly 62–67cm. Their tails grow to 40cm in length.

Weight: Male (average) 6–7kg; female (average) 5–6kg.

Description: Foxes look like small dogs and vary widely in colour and size. They can range from red to yellow to black-looking. Their most recognisable features are the white chin, underbelly and tip of the tail.

Lifespan
In the wild: On average about 2–6 years, but occasionally up to 10.
In captivity: Anywhere up to a record 15 years.

When most commonly seen: Foxes can be seen during the day but are predominantly nocturnal. Foxes do not hibernate at any time of year.

Diet: Their preferred food is small mammals, such as rabbits. However, they also eat insects to supplement their intake.

Reproduction facts: Foxes tend to breed between late December and February. The usual litter size is around 4–6 cubs, and the gestation period lasts about 2 months.

DID YOU KNOW?

Foxes can 'control' territories of up to 40km^2 in some areas.

In the UK, the golden eagle is the only natural predator of the fox.

Breeding pairs are usually monogamous; they may separate during the year but tend to reunite during the mating season.

It is actually the females who usually fight for territory, not the males.

The Golden Gosling

The Story of Eddie
the (Eagle) Gosling

'There's a baby golden eagle in my garden.'

No, there isn't.

'Right. Could you describe the chick's appearance to me please?'

'Are you doubting me?'

Yes.

'No, not at all, madam. I just need to take down all of the details so I know how best to advise you.'

Could this 'eagle chick' be the escapee from a local zoo? I wondered. No, too young. There would be no way, surely.

I went on to explain, as carefully as I could, that it was most unlikely that a young golden eagle

131

would have found its way into a domestic garden in Surrey, but she was not to be deterred.

'The chick is, without doubt, a young golden eagle. I have managed to trap it underneath an upturned bucket. If you could come and collect it, I would be most grateful.'

Sigh.

'No problem. Your address?'

The lady and her golden eagle chick were located only a short drive from the centre, so I extracted my car keys from Sam's water bowl (he knows if he hides my car keys I can't go anywhere without him) and, careful not to shake them too vigorously and thus alert their guardian, I made my way out to the car.

Curious as to what might await me, I weighed up the possibilities. The description of light, golden-coloured, downy feathers assured me that, whatever it was, it was a youngster, so I wasn't unduly worried about handling the as-yet unidentified bird.

Ten minutes later, I was faced not with a resplendent young eagle, but a twitching red bucket. Setting down the carry case I had brought with me, I knelt down and, with gloved hands, gingerly moved the bucket to unveil its mystery captive.

My first view of the golden eagle chick was … a pair of black webbed feet.

Following this first revelation came a dubious pair of knock-knees and, further, a soft-as-silk yellow belly. With the final flourish of bucket removal, there stood before me, with a wide-beaked grin, one gosling.

Now free of his B&Q-bought prison, the little chap hurried around excitedly, tripping over one or the other of his oversized feet – still vastly out of proportion to the rest of his humble frame – with every alternate step.

Once I had the playful youngster secured in my carry case, and having discussed the particulars of my find with the lady of the house (who, as she peered at me over her half-moon glasses with the scrutiny of a school headmistress addressing a caught-out youth, clearly didn't believe a single word I was saying), I set out on the short journey back to Wildlife Aid.

After a thorough examination back at the hospital, Sara had given new patient 'Eddie' a clean bill of health, and so the process of his rearing and eventual rehabilitation began. As with all of our water-bird youngsters, Eddie was initially kept in a heated incubator in the ICU, before being moved into a small pen in the second hospital. It was in his hospital pen that he spent many days 'practising' his swimming (i.e. splashing around, much to the amusement of his giggling duckling neighbours, and the snuffled objections of a hedgehog across the way) in the water tray provided.

At four weeks old, when Eddie was deemed ready (and the hospital's floor was a veritable indoor swimming bath), he was moved to the top pond, where, as is usually the case at Wildlife Aid, he was immediately taken under the proverbial and literal wing of our resident foster goose, Percy.

To allow the two to get used to each other, Eddie spent his first day away from the confines of the hospital in a run located just next to the pond. Percy's curiosity was immediately aroused at such an imposition on 'his land' and, beak held high, he instigated the direct investigation of this unprecedented arrival. Followed by a procession of his trusty web-footed militia, he waddled importantly over to Eddie's run. As he ducked and bobbed his head between the gosling and in the direction of his inquisitive private army, his orders were dealt and understood.

As Eddie stumbled free of his temporary enclosure the next morning, Percy was waiting.

Although Wildlife Aid's ethos is strictly against keeping healthy animals in captivity, Percy and his friends are all but 'resident' at the centre. There is absolutely nothing to stop any of our water birds from leaving at any time, but they choose not to 'fly the nest' owing to the ready supply of food, water facilities and overnight shelter!

Swiftly absorbing the ways of the web-footed ones during the day, and with Percy present and correct at the door to the youngster's aviary at 'letting-out time' each morning, the young apprentice thrived in his mentor's care.

As spring rolled eagerly into summer, and summer lazily into autumn, Eddie seemed to become increasingly interested in the flocks of his kind as they soared overhead on their annual pilgrimage, bound for warmer climes. One day in early October, a particularly vocal skein of migrating Canada geese flew directly over the centre, to a grounded ovation of honks and quacks. This was to be the day that Eddie left Percy's side.

Joining in with the uproarious chorus, Eddie spread his wings in preparation for takeoff. After a short propelling run, with Percy stoically watching on, he was in the air and taking up his place in the familiar V formation of the geese.

CANADA GOOSE FACT FILE

Name Canada goose (*Branta canadensis*)
Class Aves
Order Anseriformes
Family Anatidae
Terms Male – gander; female – goose;
young – gosling

Distribution (globally): Canada geese are native to North America but have been introduced to Britain and Scandinavia.

Habitat: They inhabit large bodies of water, such as lakes, reservoirs and sea fronts. Canada geese are grazers, so are often found on grass.

Size: Typically, Canada geese grow to 90–100cm in length, with a wingspan of 160–180cm.

Weight: About 4–6kg.

Description: Canada geese have long black necks and black heads, with a white throat patch. Their bodies are a grey/brown colour, with a paler underpart. Young geese have duller-coloured necks and heads, and a brownish throat area.

Lifespan
In the wild: Usually 15–20 years.
In captivity: Up to 30 years.

When most commonly seen: Canada geese can be seen all year round.

Diet: They typically eat plants, seeds and aquatic vegetation.

Reproduction facts: Canada geese pair for life; they breed around early April. The female tends to lay 5–6 eggs but it can be anywhere as high as 11. She then incubates the eggs for approximately 30 days. The young fledge in around 9 weeks, but remain with the parents through winter.

DID YOU KNOW?

A group of geese found on land or in water is called a 'gaggle'; however, a group of geese in the air is called a 'skein'.

Adult geese moult in the summer months, losing their flight feathers. This renders them flightless for about a month.

Canada geese were first introduced to the UK in 1665.

They fly at an altitude of between 300 and 915m and travel in the recognisable V formation to reduce air resistance. This enables them to travel longer distances than they would be able to fly individually.

Bedroom Yard

The Story of Callum's
Adopted Pheasant Family

'It's just a stupid pheasant,' he said sulkily, and I had to concede he had a very valid point: pheasants are, undeniably, notoriously stupid. God knows how many, on country lanes too many to recall, had nonsensically altered their course from a path that led to the immediate safety of the undergrowth, in favour of walking out directly in front of my car. But, in exchanging the most fleeting of glances with the mother of the seven-year-old boy who stood before me (visible, by virtue of his lowered baseball cap, only from the top lip down), I was in no doubt at all that this particular 'stupid pheasant' was, in fact, a very important 'stupid pheasant' indeed to its young rescuer.

Callum, on his way home from school the previous week, had found the young brood of six chicks scratching around the lifeless body of their mother. Stooping down on the grassy verge of the dirt road, he could see that there was no hope at all for the hen (female pheasant), because, judging by her injuries, she'd been killed instantly by the vehicle that had hit her. Emptying the contents of his earlier devoured lunch box into his school bag (double-checking first that there was no sneaky chocolate remainder to be had), he gently caught up each of the youngsters and put them one by one into the Tupperware. Luckily – for it would have made the inside of the container airtight – Callum decided it best not to replace the lid (so the youngsters could see where they were going, he reasoned). He instead secured the weight of his rucksack squarely across both shoulders, and opted to carry the open-topped box, with its curious cargo of six bobbing heads, out in front of him for the five minutes that it would take him to get home.

By teatime, completely unknown to the rest of his family, Callum had installed a most elaborate enclosure for his recently adopted young brood within the confines of his bedroom. Over the next few days, Callum was either at school or in his room – a fact that greatly mystified his mother, as she'd confusedly wiped a thin veil of dust from the abandoned PlayStation in the front room. Having fed his charges on a mixture of breadcrumbs and birdseed that he'd carefully emptied into his pockets from his elderly neighbour's bird table at any available opportunity, Callum was pleased with their progress.

By Day Four of parenthood, however, all was not well. One of the little chicks had separated itself from its siblings and seemed somehow sluggish in comparison with the general hubbub generated by the rest of the youngsters. Callum had kept a near-all-night vigil on the sickly chick, and, by midmorning on the Saturday, as it sat shaking ever so slightly with its eyes closed, he was sufficiently worried enough to break his silence.

Seeing his face stained by tears Callum had been too preoccupied even to notice, his mother didn't hesitate to follow her son upstairs upon his beckoned summons.

Utterly aghast at the sight of her son's bedroom farmyard, Callum's mother was temporarily at a bit of a loss as to how to react. Soon, though, the two were kneeling before the youngsters' makeshift pen, all eyes on the quiet little bird, whose head was tucked back dejectedly under its stubby juvenile little wing.

Callum's mother had called Wildlife Aid's helpline straight away.

Now, holding the sixth chick in my hand, feeling

its barely perceptible heart rate slow and regarding its extreme lethargy, I knew that there was nothing that could be done. I'd seen this too many times before. Call it 'natural selection', 'survival of the fittest', but sometimes there seems neither rhyme nor reason, and, no matter what you do, there are lives that can't be saved.

I squatted down beside Callum and, placing one hand reassuringly on his back, held out the fading chick in the other for him to stroke as I tried to explain that it was nothing that he had, or hadn't, done.

I briefly recalled my father positioning a pigeon that had long since expired – and was in fact as stiff as a board – in just such a way that he could jiggle it from beneath to give the hysterical young girl who had brought it in an illusion of hope for its miraculous recovery.

I could see in an instant that this kind of tactic would just not wash with Callum; he was a sensitive soul who would not be fooled, and so I would not try to fool him.

The young chick died in my hands.

After a moment's respectful silence, I turned to the five remaining chicks. 'Without you,' I said sincerely to Callum, 'none of these little ones would have survived. You've saved their lives.' My praise was received stoically with a sad smile.

Having seen his surrogate children settled into their new incubated housing in the Wildlife Aid ICU, Callum and his mum left for home looking forward to the day when the chicks would be old enough to be collected and released in the field behind their house.

The five pheasant chicks – fed on a diet of chick crumbs and grain – were successfully reared at the centre over the weeks that followed. They progressed from the ICU to an indoor pen, and eventually into the centre's fruit cage, where, four months later, Callum arrived to collect them. Five sleek, healthy pheasants were duly released back into the wild later that day by the young man to whom they owed their lives.

PHEASANT FACT FILE

Name   Pheasant (*Phasianus colchicus*)
Class   Aves
Order   Galliformes
Family   Phasianidae

Distribution (globally): The pheasant is found across Britain, Western Europe and

Asia, and it has recently been introduced to other areas.

Habitat: Pheasants are found in woodlands, gardens, parks and other open fields that have wooded areas nearby.

Size: Males usually grow to 70–90cm long, including the tail. Females tend to be a bit smaller, 50–70cm. Most of this size discrepancy is made up by the difference in tail lengths. Both sexes have a wingspan of around 70–90cm.

Weight: Male, 1–2kg; female, 750g–1.5kg.

Description: Pheasants are a reddish brown colour, with brown and black markings. They have a dark, iridescent green head, with a red face. They have long tails with similar markings to the body. Females are slightly lighter-coloured.

Lifespan
In the wild: 7 years.
In captivity: Up to 15 years.

When most commonly seen: All year round.

Diet: Pheasants eat a variety of foods, including seeds, insects, leaves and fruit.

Reproduction facts: Females lay their eggs during April. The size of a brood is usually 7–12 eggs. It is only the female who looks after the eggs, as the males breed with multiple partners. The eggs are incubated for around 28 days, and the chicks become fully fledged after about 2 weeks.

DID YOU KNOW?

Pheasants are originally an Asian species and were introduced to Britain by the Romans.

Pheasants can fly at speeds of 60–77kph.

Females hide their nests in long grass of up to 10m high!

Pop Goes the Weasel

The Story of Pop
the Weasel

I'd never seen Sara actually bounce before. Clawing for thephone on which I was trying to conduct an adult conversation, like one of the centre's younger fox cubs jostling for position among its siblings for a coveted suckle of bottle, the woman was practically vibrating! After shutting myself in my office (complete with ousted veterinary nurse, nose pressed to window), I could finally hear myself think. The gentleman on the other end of the line informed me that he had come across a pair of what he thought (having consulted an Internet nature site) to be baby weasels.

The pair had been somewhat unceremoniously deposited on his doormat immediately upon the

nonchalant entry of his cat through the cat flap that morning. Sadly, the smaller of the two had already met its untimely demise at the cruel jaws of the feline. The other, however, had had a miraculous escape and, quite literally, hit the ('Welcome'-matted) ground running. A scene like something from a *Carry On* film had ensued, as the bemused homeowner tore around the kitchen after the nimble little chap in a self-confessed 'decidedly *un*-nimble' fashion. With the crashing of various items of kitchenware still ringing in his ears, he had boxed the youngster and dialled Wildlife Aid's phone number.

Sara had taken the call and, her expertise being needed elsewhere in the centre, had used every feminine wile she possessed to assure the weasel's admittance to 'her' hospital before reluctantly patching the call through to me. Having finished whatever task was required of her, she had now utilised her coffee break to make her feelings known in the form of the half a dozen Post-it notes that were rapidly multiplying on my window: 'I love WEASELS!'; 'We've never had a weasel here!'; 'I'll go and pick it up!'; 'I REALLY love weasels!'; 'Pick up skirt from dry cleaners' (I suspected this one was intended for her own personal use as opposed to my window); 'I know LOADS [underlined four times] about weasels' – and so on and so on.

As Paul's car swung into the centre's car park an hour later, Sara was there to meet her eagerly awaited new patient. Instantly christened 'Pop' for obvious reasons, the young weasel was no more than three weeks old, measuring roughly 13cm from nose to tail. Given its tender age, the youngster would only just have opened its eyes, and would require two-hourly feeds of milk substitute between the hours of 6 a.m. and midnight – weasels are not nocturnal, and so would not be fed through the night by their parents out in the wild. Pop, although remarkably unscathed, was cold upon his arrival and consequently put straight into one of the ICU's incubators to warm up while Sara kept a watchful eye on him.

Setting off the large majority of the centre's alarms as she did so, (some semblance of) Sara arrived at the hospital at the unprecedented hour of 5.45 a.m. the following day to check on, and feed, Wildlife Aid's new patient. Under her care, Pop, by lunchtime, was lapping from his bowl all by himself. Over the next few days, mashed dog food would be added to the milk substitute in his bowl, and following the dog food, once the young kit's teeth were fully grown, tiny pieces of chick for him to nibble on.

Pop's chief place of residence during his stay at the centre was the simulated weasel hole of Sara's sleeve. In the wild, weasels don't actually dig their own burrows, preferring to occupy the abandoned abode of a rabbit or similar. Sara's sleeve was the perfect borrowed abode for Pop: dark, warm and tunnel-shaped.

However, like their distant relative the skunk, weasels, if panicked, will release a putrid smell from their anal scent glands. Sara's young stowaway, while sleeping soundly one afternoon, got spooked by the bark of a distant dog and, needless to say, Pop was evicted without further notice.

In the four months Pop was with us, the little weasel kept Wildlife Aid's volunteers constantly amused with his acrobatics and cheeky antics and, to this day, remains a firm favourite among all those who cared for him throughout his stay.

Unbeknown to Pop – as he performed his usual trick of shooting up one of the volunteers' sleeves while she attempted to top up his food bowl, only to reappear moments later from the other – 1 September was to be a big day.

For the last week, Wildlife Aid's own 'man who can', Graham, had been squirrelling away in the workshop creating what he assured all who would listen (and several who wouldn't) was to be a masterpiece. After a week of suspicious bangs and clatters, Graham emerged with 'the Pop Box'. A bespoke hedgehog box, the little weasel's new accommodation was fit for a king, with its specially insulated bedroom quarters leading into a spacious outdoor run. The idea was that food could be dropped into a surreptitious trapdoor at the top of the box as Pop slept, so that his contact with humans would be negligible, ensuring, in time, a successful rehabilitation back into the wild.

The Pop Box was installed under a hedgerow in the orchard of the centre's grounds and, once Pop had acclimatised to his new surroundings over the course of a week or so, Sara and I waited until nightfall, whereupon we sneaked out to detach the run section of his enclosure so that, when he awoke in the morning, the world would be his oyster.

Since his release, there have been several sightings of Pop, who, true to his name, has an uncanny knack of popping up wherever and whenever you least expect him, from intangibly small gaps in the ground to cracks in the woodwork of disused aviaries!

And, as for Sara's incorrigible charm, not only did Pop find his way to our door, but so too did the member of the public who found him. Paul is now a regular and most valuable volunteer at Wildlife Aid.

WEASEL FACT FILE

Name	Weasel (*Mustela nivalis*)
Class	Mammalia
Order	Carnivora
Family	Mustelidae
Terms	Male – hob; female – jill; young – kit; group – gang or sneak

Distribution (globally): Weasels can be found throughout Britain, Europe, North Africa, Asia and North America and have been recently introduced to New Zealand.

Habitat: Weasels are very versatile animals, living almost anywhere they can find shelter and food, including grasslands, woodlands, farmlands, sand dunes and even mountains.

Size: Males have a body length of about 18–22cm, with a tail of roughly 4–6cm. Females are slightly smaller, with a body length of 17–19cm and a tail of 3–5cm.

Weight: Males, 100–130g; females, 50–80g.

Description: Weasels have a long slender

body, brown in colour, with a white underpart. They have a short tail and legs, rounded ears and black eyes.

Lifespan
In the wild: Up to 3 years.
In captivity: Up to 10 years.

When most commonly seen: Weasels can be seen at any time of day, and during any part of the year.

Diet: Weasels have to eat every 24 hours. They feed on small rodents, rabbits, birds and eggs.

Reproduction facts: The weasel becomes sexually mature after 3 to 4 months. Breeding season is in early spring; the gestation period for weasels is around 35–37 days. A typical litter size is 4–6 kits, but it can be as many as 10. The male weasel takes no part in parenting the young. The kits are weaned after 4 weeks; by 12 weeks they are efficient killers and the family unit splits up.

DID YOU KNOW?

Historically, weasels were believed to have magic powers. Supposedly, they could bring their dead back to life and hypnotise their prey by dancing.

The weasel is the smallest carnivore in the world.

Males can control territories as large as 40 acres.

A Bird in the Hand

The Story of Stig
the Herring Gull

It was completely by chance that I happened to call a friend, Richard, from another rescue centre in the coastal village of Fairlight, near Hastings, one summer's afternoon. We 'wildlife types' will often 'check in' with one another, comparing notes on the recent goings-on of our various centres and their current residents. Ironically, although our voices are so familiar to each other, few of us have actually met face to face, never quite able to coordinate our ever-changing, animal-dictated schedules.

I had been meaning to visit the centre Richard worked at for some time (a rather embarrassing five years, actually), since Fairlight was where I used

to spend my childhood holidays in a caravan with my parents.

Dealing mainly with seabirds and seals (in addition to the same assorted array of species that pass through Wildlife Aid's own doors), Richard was filling me in on a recent jaunt that had led him practically past my door. A seal had strayed from its herd, and been found in a degree of disoriented distress near the Chertsey lock of the Thames. After its successful capture and subsequent healing stay in Fairlight, the recuperated mammal was now ready to be returned to the sea. Because I'd shown interest in the seal's recovery, Richard asked if I would like to escape the 'Surrey wilds' for a day to accompany him on the release the next morning. I laughed, Richard laughed, and, promising we'd speak again in the not too distant future, we said our goodbyes.

Later that day, Sara and I completed our rounds with 'Stig'. Extending to me his usual greeting (pinching a minute section of my skin in his beak, and then sharply twisting it for added emphasis), Stig seemed to be in fine form. Having spent three or four months with us, the gull's plumage was now completely waterproof – we'd tried and tested this point thoroughly, it being vital for the safe release of any seabird – and his wingspan was a good 120cm (another good gauge of when a herring gull is ready for release).

'It's a shame we can't get him to the coast really,' Sara mused as she went about separating Stig's beak and my skin – a procedure that had become something of a routine following the gull's regular check-ups. There are in fact, contrary to popular belief, as many seagulls inland as there are on the coast, but I knew what she meant; it was a nice notion.

I thought back to the young herring gull's rescue ...

The local council tip would not have been one of my first choices of location for passing the time on what had been one of the hottest days of the year. However, duty had called, or, rather, the chief refuse officer had called. It was 'removal day' and, in clearing out a large portion of the site, a couple of the men had come across a baby herring gull. They didn't know what to do with the youngster, but it would have to be moved, for in a matter of moments the sharp steel claws of the colossal digger would be tearing their way through the very surface on which the humble little one stood and, feeling sure that the fluffy little chick was far too young to be left on its own, they had decided to scoop up the lost-looking soul in a spare hardhat and deliver it to their boss's office.

Such a plan, in itself, had seemed fairly straightforward. Not so, however, when you factor into the equation a fiercely protective mother gull.

Gladder than ever of their own safety attire, the two would-be rescuers endured numerous dive-bombings from Mrs Gull as they tried to round up the deceptively agile young seagull.

Upon our arrival, with the hardhat and its occupant under one arm, I (well, actually, cameraman Jim!) had set out on the tricky ascent of the mountain of random debris – the stench, by now, consuming parts of my being that I hadn't even known existed prior to their sensory invasion. Directed by the men who'd found the gull, I (Jim) placed the cheeping bird back within the vicinity of where it had been found, but on a safer patch that wasn't due to be cleared for a further month.

Hiding behind a wall comprising, among other things, a chagrinned (probably at the audacity of being superseded) dishwasher, a decomposing time-greened flan and a very dejected, suspiciously staring (through her one remaining eye, anyway) doll, we'd waited.

At around the point where the flan had begun to look appealing, I'd realised that the mother herring gull wasn't going to return. There was no way we could have left the youngster any longer in such heat: he would have dehydrated, starved or been snatched by an opportunistic cat.

As soon as he arrived at the hospital, swapping hardhat for incubator, the young gull was immediately fed on a bowl of pond-water-soaked whitebait. Gulls are particularly quick to catch on when it comes to picking up food for themselves, and, after a couple of tweezers-fed meals, with the tweezers lingering ever closer to the bowl of fish, the young seabird was soon pecking at his meals all by himself.

As one of our most 'low-maintenance' inmates, species-wise, the gull progressed up the Wildlife Aid rehabilitation procedure ladder resiliently. When he was a month old, the size of his meals (sprats by this time, rather than whitebait) had grown with him, until twelve weeks later, when, although still a juvenile mottled brown and white in colour, his downy fluff was gradually replaced by adult 'primary', or 'flight' feathers, and he was moved to a larger area within the centre.

... Stig and I, now extricated from each other, set about the rest of the afternoon: for him, sprats; for me, the general running of Wildlife Aid. Back in my office, as I glanced over my diary for the following day, it struck me as uncanny that so many of the centre's staff were to be present at the same time: one vet, two vet nurses, two of our most experienced rescuers and a full rota of volunteers. Was someone trying to tell me something? I picked up the phone and dialled Richard's number.

A Bird in the Hand

The next morning, feeling bemused and a little surplus, I found myself in my car en route to Fairlight. Sara had assured me she was in complete control (a notion that made me itch slightly), and that both Stig and I could do with filling our lungs with fresh sea air.

It was a mystical morning in Fairlight. Sea met sky elusively behind a veil of mist, such that the beach's final row of pebbles appeared to define the edge of the world.

Prior to our standing before the tide, Richard had secured a ring around Stig's bandy ankle, and a plastic tag through the flipper of the seal in order to monitor them. Now, assembled before the gently lulling surf, it was time to furnish sea and sky with returning fin and first flight respectively. As Richard and his crew waded into the water, the seal's weight suspended between them in a carrying sling, I unfastened Stig's cage and carefully lifted him from its confines. With one cursory 'pinch 'n' twist', Stig spread his wings and, mirrored by his flippered counterpart below, allowed his body to be swept up and away by the current.

HERRING GULL FACT FILE

Name	Herring gull (*Larus argentatus argenteus*)
Class	Aves
Order	Charadriiformes
Family	Laridae

Distribution (globally): Herring gulls inhabit Britain, Europe, North Africa, Northern Asia and North America.

Habitat: Herring gulls live in a variety of habitats, such as cliffs, beaches, islands and buildings.

Size: Females are slightly smaller than males. A male herring gull is about 55–65cm in length, and has a wingspan of about 150cm.

Weight: 750g–1.5kg.

Description: Herring gulls have white underparts and grey tops. Their heads are white, though in the autumn develop brown spots. Their beak is a bright yellow with a red spot on it. They have pink legs with webbed feet. Young gulls are a greyish brown colour.

Lifespan
In the wild: Up to 30 years.
In captivity: The oldest recorded herring gull in captivity was 44 years old.

When most commonly seen: They tend to stay around the coasts of Britain, and move inland during the winter.

Diet: Herring gulls are omnivorous. Although they are typically fish eaters, they have become resourceful and opportunistic scavengers. They will eat almost anything discarded in rubbish tips and on the ground. These gulls will also eat insects, amphibians, birds' eggs and small mammals and have even been known to eat snakes.

Reproduction facts: Herring gulls become sexually mature after about 3 years. They breed in colonies and so return in spring to fight for their territory. Both the male and female bird incubate the brood, which usually has 2–6 eggs. The chicks hatch after 30 days and are fully fledged within 40 days after that.

DID YOU KNOW?
Chicks obtain meals by pecking at the red spot on their parent's bill. This encourages the parent to regurgitate food for them.

Herring gull populations have decreased by 50 per cent in the last 30 years. There are now only 10 breeding sites throughout the UK.

During the nineteenth century, herring gulls almost became extinct in North America as their feathers were such collectable items.

Squirrel v Birdfeeder

The Story of Squiggle
the Squirrel

I swung my silver steed (Volvo) into the designated driveway, only narrowly missing a garish red and yellow (flat-tyred) tricycle, and manoeuvred my way through the further chicanes of a well-bludgeoned football, several regrettable Anne Boleyns of the doll kingdom and numerous remote-controlled (evidently *un*controllable) cars.

Picking my way carefully over the colourful carnage, I headed in the general direction of the front door and, having rung the bell, stepped back and surveyed the lawn behind me – veritable Toys 'R' Us jungle that it was. At the sound of the door's complaining hinges, I turned around ready to address … well, absolutely no one, or so I thought.

As I lowered my gaze a metre or so, my bemused eyes met their audience: a buzzing gaggle of chocolate-covered faces. Just as I was about to introduce myself, a harassed-looking lady appeared in the hallway, tea towel in one hand, child trailing from the other.

'Simon?' she enquired.

I nodded.

As I followed her through the somewhat chaotic house, she explained to me that it was the day of her son's sixth birthday party – a fact already fairly evident to me in the form of the pack of young children who had attached themselves like limpets to each of my legs, considerably slowing my progress. The kids had been running riot in the back garden, she said, when one had noticed a 'squiggle' dangling from the birdfeeder.

I silently cursed the existence of such birdfeeders. These days, it would seem that most are made more as decorative garden ornaments than practical bird-food providers. With their glamorous wrought-iron arms folding and looping in all directions, they are nothing more than a contrived, ill-conceived display of modern art – aesthetically pleasing to the owner, a potentially lethal trap for wildlife. The trouble is that, invariably, any two of these iron 'arms' tend to narrow to a sharp V shape as they taper into the main frame of the birdfeeder.

There are not many contraptions that would pose a challenge to the agile squirrel that is partial to a bit of bird food, but I wish I had a penny for every time I'd heard the story that, I was certain, I was about to be told.

'It was going crazy,' she said, gesturing, throwing both arms in the air and inadvertently whipping one of the children in the eye with her tea towel, 'thrashing about, trying to free itself. I rushed over and saw that its foot was trapped in the metal bit at the top' (the dreaded V, I thought) 'but, every time I approached, it growled like a lion!' Catching her arms on a trajectory to the ceiling once more, luckily, the child had the presence of mind to duck this time. 'And please don't think me pathetic – but I just couldn't get near it for fear of losing a good few fingers!'

She was absolutely right to have called us, I assured her. Squirrels have an exceedingly nasty bite on them, one that, if I wasn't very careful, would go straight through even the thickest pair of gloves I could find to bring with me, and now clutched tightly in my hand.

Once alone in the garden, I made my way towards the birdfeeder. At first sight, the squirrel appeared defeated, hanging heavily from one hind leg, which was trapped in the metal exactly as I had imagined. In their eagerness to secure a tasty meal, like the most proficient trapeze artists, the little opportunists navigate their way towards their prize, not accounting for the slippery surface of the shiny metal. As they lose their grip, their legs slide and get caught between the iron struts, and the struggle to free themselves serves only to wedge the trapped limb deeper and deeper into the cruel V. I was unsure how long this particular little fellow had been in such a predicament, and prayed I'd got there in time. Generally, in such circumstances, the longer the animal is left, the more likely it is that the circulation in the trapped limb will become completely cut off, or, worse still, as a result of violent struggling, the leg or foot will be broken.

Quickening my step, I was relieved to see the youngster's muscles tense as it swung out at me, holding its body weight as if in some sort of advanced yoga position. Its beady eyes were wide and fixed on me; it was growling softly, warning me to stay back.

I glanced over my shoulder at the row of noses pressed on the glass of the sliding double doors to the house, each transfixed expression silently willing me to come off worse in my acrimonious encounter with the squirrel, and thus result in a juicy bloodbath anecdote for later playground use and embellishment.

Talking in what I hoped were soothing hushed

tones to the terrified creature, I set down my carry case on the grass, and reached one gloved hand behind its head, scruffing it just behind its jaw to prevent it from whipping its head and long sharp teeth around to bite me. Making sure my grip was firm but not overpowering, I used my other hand to force apart the iron bars, while at the same time easing the youngster upwards to free its ensnared foot.

The young squirrel was voicing its objection loudly, its whole body trembling from a mixture of tension and fear as I raised it, as gently as I could, from the formidable vice. Feeling its heart pounding wildly through the dense material of my glove, I set the little fellow's hind legs on the floor, and to my great relief saw that the previously trapped foot was paddling at the earth with a full range of movement, and therefore not broken.

Rapturous applause broke out from the lady of the house as I made my way back up the garden with the youngster safely in my carry case. I couldn't help but be a little disappointed as the children's reaction came into view: at the site of no gore, they appeared indisputably miffed.

'Squiggle' spent the next 24 hours at the centre, until we were absolutely sure that there was indeed no damage done to his foot, and, following this period of R&R, he

was returned whence he came. The disgraced birdfeeder
was consigned to a dusty corner of the garage.

SQUIRREL FACT FILE

Name Grey squirrel (*Sciurus carolinensis*)
Class Mammalia
Order Rodentia
Family Sciuridae

Distribution (globally): The grey squirrel can
be found across most of the UK,
Italy, South Africa, Australia and its
origin the USA.

Habitat: The grey squirrel prefers broadleaved
woodlands; however, it is very adaptable to
most environments and is found in most
woods, parks and gardens.

Size: A grey squirrel is about 20–30cm tall
(head and body), with a tail between 15 and
25cm long.

Weight: 400–700g.

Description: Grey squirrels are predominantly grey-coloured with a lighter underside. They have smaller ear tufts than red squirrels, but are generally larger in size. Both males and females look alike.

Lifespan
In the wild: Approximately 9 years.
In captivity: Up to 12 years.

When most commonly seen: Squirrels are most active from sunrise to sunset. In autumn they are particularly busy hoarding food to survive the harsh winter.

Diet: Depending on the time of year, squirrels eat a variety of foods including, seeds, nuts, flowers, shoots, fruits, insects and sometimes even birds' eggs. Squirrels bury surplus food or hide it in trees for later use.

Reproduction facts: There are two breeding periods in any year: December to February and April to May. The females become solitary during the gestation period, which lasts about 45 days. They nest in a drey, which is made from twigs.

There are usually 1–8 young in a litter, and they are weaned in 10 weeks.

DID YOU KNOW?

Grey squirrels have led to the occurrence of albino squirrels in Britain. Although the odds against the birth of a pure-white squirrel are 1 in 100,000, there have been regular sightings of them in some areas. There are also black squirrels in the UK.

Baby squirrels weigh approximately 28g at birth, and are 25mm long. They have no hair or teeth.

Grey squirrels were introduced to the UK in the late nineteenth century.

Tired and Wired

The Story of Bliss the Badger

'Ah, bliss!' I said to Sam as I sank into the accommodating comfort of my fireside chair. It had been a long, cold February day that I had thought, at several junctures, would never end. As if some universal alarm clock had sounded, it would seem that today had been the day the animal kingdom had decided to awaken from its winter's sleep. Since first light I had been on my feet, racing here and there, in pursuit of various waifs and strays in need of the centre's expertise.

The glaring digital display of the microwave had hollered 01:03 at me as I attempted to reheat (for the third time) the mug of cocoa that now warmed my hands. Raising the friendly nightcap to my lips,

its homely aroma already beginning to soothe my day's chaos, I was just about to take my first sip when: 'brrriing, brrriing!' After exchanging an exasperated glance with Sam, who (as any dog owner would testify) actually seemed to roll his eyes, before grunting and loping off in the direction of the kitchen's peaceful solitude, I reached for my insomniac mobile phone.

Forty-five minutes later I was standing in a veterinary practice in Hampshire with a distinctly bleary-eyed veterinary nurse who had evidently drawn the short straw to stay up to wait for my arrival. Dealing only with domestic animals, the staff at the surgery had been unsure of how best to treat the wild badger cub that had been rushed in by a worried member of the public.

Kneeling down by the cage, I unfastened its catch and reached in to peel back the towel that covered the frightened youngster, which was no more than five or six weeks old. I could immediately see blood coming from the cub's face. Knowing it to be far too young to inflict any sort of injury, I sat down on the concrete floor and gently positioned the cub in my lap so I could get a better look. With veterinary nurse Kate's help, I cleaned the wound enough to be able to assess the damage. There was a section at the very front of the cub's lower jaw, about an inch wide, actually hanging right off. Attached only by a thin thread of flesh, the detached portion of teeth and bone exposed a gaping wound. The cut looked straight, severed in a clean line. I couldn't imagine for the life of me how an animal could come by such an injury. An old tin can? I wondered.

And herein lies the inherent difficulty faced by all those who work in animal welfare: they can't tell you where the pain is, what sort of pain it is, how long the symptoms have been present or how the malady was procured – all the basic information ascertained by a doctor within the first minutes of treating a patient of the human variety.

Perplexed and worried, I wrapped the little cub back up in her towel for warmth, and transferred her to a carry case for the journey.

Back at the centre, to the auspicious – albeit decidedly unwelcome – melody of the dawn chorus, I administered the necessary emergency treatment, including painkillers, antibiotics and a rehydrating Hartmann's drip. These would keep our new arrival as comfortable as possible in her incubator until such an hour that it would be deemed sociable enough for me to call one of Wildlife Aid's own vets, Jim Logan. And then, regrettably, thinking it best to forgo my much-awaited cocoa (for reasons of irreparable 'curdle-age'), I finally went to bed.

At his surgery the following morning, Jim was as

mystified as I was upon examining badger cub 'Bliss'. But, with no way of knowing what horror had befallen her previously, we had to press on and do the best for her that we could. What ensued was one of the longest and, by far, most complex operations I had ever witnessed. Jim skilfully reconstructed the cub's jaw. Using a fine surgical wire, he dexterously stitched the hanging section of flesh and bone back into place. As I watched Jim work, I couldn't help but notice how very small and vulnerable the young orphan looked as she lay, defenceless and sleeping, on the operation table, surrounded by the leads and tubes of an environment that must seem so wholly alien to her.

Although the procedure went well, putting any animal, let alone a wild animal – and one so young, to boot – under general anaesthetic for a prolonged period of time carries with it a certain degree of risk. All we could do now was wait and pray for Bliss' recovery. She was to stay at Jim's surgery for the next 48 hours so he could monitor her progress and, if necessary, be on hand to administer any emergency treatment.

Bliss was a fighter. Two days later, I collected her from Jim's practice looking as bright as a button. She had been a clear favourite among the surgery's veterinary nurses for her brave recovery and heart-melting youthful curiosity, and so our departure was

no easy feat. Nor, for that matter, was our return to
Wildlife Aid – the first cub of the year is always a
popular patient at the centre. Our young badger cubs
are reared in much the same way as our fawns, in that
they require two-hourly feeds around the clock, thus
necessitating a 'foster carer' to take them home
overnight to administer such midnight meals. Bliss
was not at a loss for able volunteers to adopt her.

Bottle-fed initially, due to her poorly mouth and
consequent inability to munch solid foods, Bliss
began to gain weight and strength. A month into her
stay saw the admittance of two further orphans of a
similar age and, following the removal, by Jim, of the
supporting wires in her jaw six weeks after they'd
been put in, Bliss was integrated into the pair with
whom she'd spend the rest of her time at the centre.

*Bliss and her new brother and sister were later joined by
two more cubs to go through the centre's rehabilitation
process, which would see their collective release back
into the wild that autumn. Even though Wildlife Aid's
protocol denotes that the badgers have no contact with
humans after a certain point in their rehabilitation, Bliss
– by now a 15-kg, beautifully coated alpha female – was
always instantly recognisable to us, her bottom jaw being
half a centimetre shorter than her top, meaning that her
tongue poked out just a little!*

BADGER FACT FILE

Name	Eurasian badger (*Meles meles*)
Class	Mammal
Order	Carnivora
Family	Mustelidae
Terms	Male – boar; female – sow; young – cub; home – den or sett

Distribution (globally): Badgers inhabit most of Europe, Asia and the Far East.

Habitat: They mainly live in woodlands, but can be found on farms and in urban gardens.

Size: A male badger grows to about 70–90cm in length, with a 15cm tail. The females tend to be smaller.

Weight: Winter, 7–13kg; summer, 16–24kg.

Description: Badgers have stocky grey bodies, with black and white stripes running from their nose to their shoulders. They have white-tipped ears and a short tail.

Lifespan: Up to 14 years.

When most commonly seen: Badgers are primarily nocturnal creatures, emerging from their setts at dusk.

Diet: Badgers are omnivores. This means they will eat almost anything – meat, vegetables, nuts, roots, seeds, insects or even other dead animals. (They are also more than partial to a bit of molasses!)

Reproduction facts: Badgers become sexually mature at 14 months old; they will mate at any time between late winter and midsummer. The fertilised eggs are then suspended in the uterus of the female, without undergoing any embryonic growth, for about 10 months or until the climate conditions become ideal for cubs. The gestation period then lasts for about 7 weeks, with a resulting litter of 2–6 young.

DID YOU KNOW?

Badgers live in clans. The largest clan recorded consisted of 23 individuals. These clans can control territories of up to 400 acres.

Badger setts consist of many different chambers with specific functions such as nests, sleeping quarters and toilets.

The dominant pair of a clan is often the only pair who successfully reproduce; sometimes the dominant female will actually kill other badgers' cubs.

Badgers take nesting material out of their sett to 'air' it during the day.

Wood Splinters

The Story of Balsa the Great Spotted Woodpecker

Sandy had been out walking her ever-irrepressibly excitable golden retriever, Scooby, and bathing in the early-summer sunshine, which beat its way resplendently through the trees of the local woodland. Following the hour-long jaunt of stick throwing, lake splashing and unhealthy eating (Sandy, a Mr Whippy with flake and extra strawberry sauce; Scooby, manure), the tired duo turned the final corner of their return journey into Sandy's quiet cul-de-sac.

Even though the late-June rays had dried up the slushy mud paths that Sandy and Scooby had traipsed during the winter months, Scooby still seemed able to return from his walks in a hundred

different shades of brown. So, rather than enter her home through the front door – and straight on to her much-regretted choice of pale-cream carpet – Sandy thought it best to go through the side gate and straight into the garden with her dishevelled hound. Closing the wooden gate behind her, she paused, straining her ears to discern the odd popping noise, conspicuous by its lack of cohesion with the usual sounds of her suburban neighbourhood. It seemed to be coming from next door and sounded like a cross between muted fireworks and the sudden whoosh of a newly opened but vigorously shaken bottle of cola.

An air rifle? thought Sandy, instinctively looking up at the branches of the tall trees that lined the far side of her garden. Just as she did so, she caught sight of a muddle of black, white and red tumbling towards the ground.

Shooing Scooby away, she dashed to where the woodpecker lay – its wing bloody, and at a horrible angle – on the grass beneath. Having picked up the injured bird as carefully as she could, she snatched a fresh tea towel from the washing line and wrapped him up gently, placing him in the nearest container to hand (an empty, mesh-covered flower pot) so that she could drive him to Wildlife Aid.

I have to say that animal cruelty astounds and disgusts me in equal measures. Wayward kids taking potshots at our wildlife is, sickeningly, not that uncommon. Some of the cruelty cases that we've seen over the years would bend your bones: from hedgehog 'footballs', to a rabbit that had been 'crucified' – nailed to a fence by her paws, she had lost her fight for survival just after arriving at Wildlife Aid, having given birth to five stillborn young.

Taking the flower pot from a seething Sandy – who was still cursing the youth in question under her breath – I removed the covering mesh lid and examined the wounded bird. Being in possession of the knowledge that woodpeckers are fully independent at just ten days old, I quickly ascertained from the bird's plumage that this one was still clearly quite young. The bird's wing was undoubtedly broken. An X-ray would be able to tell me the full extent of the damage.

Bidding Sandy farewell, I took the patient up to the centre's X-ray unit. Knowing better than to anaesthetise the young bird, for birds are, in general, very highly stressed in captivity – especially breeds such as woodpeckers or kingfishers – I instead opted to don the lead-lined gloves and apron that would assure my safety as I held the bird still during its X-ray.

With the developed X-ray plate in my hand a few minutes later, I was able to tell that the radius and ulna were broken. The fractures were clean, though, and, luckily, not too close to the joint – which would have made splinting the injury difficult, if not impossible.

With Hazel's help, using some Elastoplast, I strapped the bird's damaged wing to its body – to manipulate and splint the wing would require anaesthetic, and the shocked young bird just wasn't strong enough yet.

For the couple of days that followed, 'Balsa' was treated with antibiotics and painkillers, and force-fed four times a day on a staple diet of Sluis (bird-food mix), cat food and meal worms covered in honey (a woodpecker favourite!).

Balsa seemed all the better for 48 hours of honey-coated 'R&R', and so came the time to treat the youngster's wing. Preparing all the necessary instruments first, so as to keep to a bare minimum the length of time that the bird had to be anaesthetised, we set to work manipulating the delicate bones of Balsa's wing into realignment before splinting it. Again, after strapping the repaired wing once more to the young woodpecker's body with Elastoplast, we hurriedly took one more X-ray of the wing while the bird was still under anaesthetic, to be sure that the bones were correctly set. Satisfied that this was the case, Hazel and I anxiously awaited Balsa's awakening.

Moments later, the groggy woodpecker – looking as if he was experiencing the after-effects of a heavy night out on the town – slowly came to, one eye at a time. An hour or two later, young Balsa was gratefully guzzling down his dinner and entertaining Hazel by shinning up the sleeve of her jumper, displaying admiral balance for one temporarily mono-winged!

Balsa's splint was left on for two weeks while his wounds healed, whereupon Hazel removed the bandages to assess how well the fractures had fused. Sufficiently well healed, the young woodpecker was then confined in a small cage for a further week, and finally moved to a larger aviary for flight practice. Three weeks later Balsa was released back into the wild, a perfectly able-winged woodpecker.

WOODPECKER FACT FILE

Name Great spotted woodpecker
(*Dendrocopos major*)
Class Aves
Order Piciformes
Family Picidae

Distribution (globally): The great spotted woodpecker is found around Britain, Europe, Asia and North Africa.

Habitat: They inhabit all kinds of woodland, gardens and parks.

Size: They are about 20–25cm in length and have a wingspan of up to 45cm.

Weight: They are very light birds, weighing around just 90g.

Description: Great spotted woodpeckers have predominantly black and white feathers. They have a white underpart and a white patch on each wing. Both male and female birds have a red patch under the tail, though it's only the male that has a red spot on its nape. Young birds look very similar to adults, though they have a bright red cap on their heads.

Lifespan
In the wild: About 11 years.
In captivity: Up to 13 years.

When most commonly seen: All year round.

Diet: They eat a variety of foods, including insects, seeds, nuts and sometimes other birds' eggs.

Reproduction facts: The breeding season begins around late March and continues through June. After pairing up, both the male and female 'hack' out a nesting chamber in a tree. Both parents incubate the brood, which typically consists of 4 to 7 eggs. The chicks hatch after 2 weeks and become fully independent after just 10 days.

DID YOU KNOW?

The great spotted woodpecker can eat all the seeds from a pine cone in under four minutes, using up to 800 blows to achieve this. That's just over three blows per second!

They can locate the positions of grubs in trees by tapping on the tree and listening for hollow tunnels.

When woodpeckers climb trees, their feet and the feathers in their tail form a tripod, which helps them to stick to the surface. Their feathers are uniquely resilient and thus provide very strong support.

Grey Days

The Story of Goldie
the Pigeon

I cannot iterate enough how I wish people would be more mindful of their litter. The case in point huddled before me in a forlorn little bundle of dejected defeat.

It was a distinctly grey day that found me crouched down on my haunches beneath an equally grey and unpicturesque industrial railway bridge beside the form of a bedraggled young pigeon.

Angus – remembering that he had seen my car, with its 'Wildlife Aid Ambulance' sticker on the side, parked up outside the bakery that had become my regular lunchtime haunt – had doubled back at a sprint, leaving his girlfriend under the bridge with the injured young bird, that they had stumbled across, wrapped up in her jacket.

GREY DAYS

I exited the bakery, looking forward very much to getting back to the centre and consuming the piping-hot chilli soup that was exuding all manner of tantalising spicy aromas from the neatly packed brown-paper bag in my hand. (I very rarely had the time to devour such a culinary treat – usually a sandwich munched in the car en route to a rescue was the order of the day.) As I paused to cross the road, I spotted a young man agitatedly pacing up and down beside my car, scanning the area all about him in anticipation of tracking down the driver to the wildlife ambulance that he'd sought out. Catching my eye as I approached, he jogged over gratefully to close the gap between us. He introduced himself and quickly went on to explain the reason for his vigil of my car.

Soon the two of us were hotfooting it down towards the bridge, my soup ruefully replaced by carry case and Wildlife Aid 'kit box'. On arrival at the scene I knelt down beside Angus's girlfriend, Sarah, who gently produced the shivering young pigeon from beneath the folds of her woollen coat. Taking the young bird from her and cupping its slight form in my palms, I was immediately shocked by what I saw: the squab (young pigeon) had somehow managed to get a plastic 'locking ring' – of the sort you might find on the neck of a juice or water bottle to seal the gap between the bottle itself and the cap – stuck in its beak beneath its tongue and around the back of its head, like a horse's bridle. The plastic ring had already cut into the fleshy corners of the bird's beak and was burning a nasty patch into the back of its neck.

For its winged lack of hands, the bird had obviously struggled relentlessly in its attempts to try to free itself. The second I touched the plastic ring, however, it popped off easily, over the youngster's head.

'Oh!' exclaimed Sarah, wincing. 'I didn't dare touch it in case I did even more damage,' she concluded apologetically.

Settling the youngster within a towel into my carry case, knowing that its wounds would need treating back at the hospital, I set about reassuring her. 'You did exactly the right thing,' I said. 'If in doubt, keep an injured bird warm, dark and quiet, and call a wildlife centre such as ours – either your local branch of the RSPCA, or local police should be able to give you details of such an organisation if you're unsure.'

Sarah smiled appreciatively and, having bid her 'rescuee' a fringe-obscured but, I quietly suspected, slightly tearful farewell, she and Angus were on their way. I headed back towards my car, turning around briefly to see Angus put a comforting arm around his girlfriend's shoulders.

Back at the hospital, one of our veterinary nurses, Hazel, carefully dabbed some soothing Fuciderm gel around the squab's beak and, as I held the young bird still, administered a dose of oral painkiller, Metacam. Judging by the fluffy golden tufts that still largely obscured the grey adult plumage that was beginning to come through beneath, 'Goldie' could have been no more than three weeks old. For a further few days, the youngster would be kept on the oral antibiotic Baytril, and would be tube-fed on a special liquid hand-rearing diet for birds until it was old enough to pick up food for itself.

Back in my office, having resignedly retrieved my now more chilly than chilli soup from the car, I dialled the number Angus had jotted down for me, and left a message at the sound of Sarah's automated invitation. I explained that the patient, having been treated for his injuries, was calm and settled in our ICU. Thanking her and Angus for sparing their time to help the young nestling, I cited the relevant details for her to quote should she wish to call the centre to check on its progress.

At around nine weeks old, his wounds totally healed, Goldie was put into an aviary with a group of seven other young pigeons, together with whom he would learn to fly, pick up food and weather the outdoor conditions that a life back in the wild would surely bring.

A month later saw Sarah and me, against a considerably bluer sky, setting free an eight-strong flock of fully fledged, healthy young pigeons from atop the bridge where Goldie was originally found.

PIGEON FACT FILE

Name	Feral pigeon (*Columba livia*)
Class	Aves
Order	Columbiformes
Family	Columbidae
Terms	Male – cock; female – hen; young – squab; home – nest

Distribution (globally): Pigeons are found all over Europe, Africa, North and South America and Asia.

Habitat: Pigeons usually nest on cliffs, or other structures resembling cliffs, such as ledges on buildings.

Size: Usually between 30 and 35cm from head to tail, with a wingspan of 60–70cm.

Weight: 300–350g.

Description: Pigeons can be a variety of colours. They are generally grey but have iridescent feathers on the neck (called a hackle), which shine green, purple and yellow in the light. Some pigeons are brown or white. Males and females look alike, but the male's hackle is more iridescent than the female's. They have orange eyes.

Lifespan
In the wild: 3–5 years.
In captivity: About 15 years (however, the oldest recorded lived to 35!).

When most commonly seen: All year round.

Diet: Pigeons mainly eat seeds, but they will feed on most things they can find, such as meat and bread.

Reproduction facts: The female usually lays two white eggs. Both the male and female take it in turns to incubate the eggs, and this lasts for a period of around 18 days, until the eggs hatch.

DID YOU KNOW?

Usually birds take a sip of water and throw back their heads to let the water trickle down their throats. Pigeons, on the other hand, suck up water using their beaks like straws.

Pigeons require 15 per cent of their body weight in fresh water per day.

Both male and female pigeons produce 'pigeon milk' to feed their young. This 'milk' is produced in the pigeons' crop.

Pigeons are superb fliers and can reach speeds of up to 80kph.

'There's a Moose Loose ...'

The Story of Hickorydickorydock the Wood Mouse

I loosened my tie and, tilting my head back, snapped open the top button of my shirt collar. Ah, air! So unaccustomed was I to wearing a suit after 25 years out of my city job that now finding myself trapped within the confines of one steeped me in a deep sense of foreboding. Although I would be glad to get home and once more take up residence in my Wildlife Aid 'uniform' of jeans and sweatshirt, the day had in fact been a joyous one – my cousin's wedding, no less.

Following the M25's course to the centre while reflecting on the afternoon's highlights, I tried to recall my last 'day off'. Mentally flicking through 2005, 2004 and 2003, and coming up with nothing,

I decided that, for the sake of argument, it had been a while.

Time appeared to slow as I turned my key in the lock of the farmhouse door. It was a bit like the first few seconds after waking – the delightful serene nothingness of being before reality crashes back into form. The click of the lock, the squeak of decrepit hinges, silence. Then, '*WOOF, WOOF, WOOF!*'; '*Brrriing, brrriing!*'; 'Daaaddd! shut the *door* – it's b****y *freeeeeezzing!*' A veritable forest of Post-it notes fluttered around in the indoor tornado.

Reality.

Amid the general confusion, I opted first for the phone. Cradling the receiver on my shoulder, I simultaneously managed to push the door to with one foot, and stroke as many dogs as my mere mortal two-handed limit would allow.

The call was not the easiest to fathom, punctuated, as it was, by hysterical yelps. I eventually ascertained that there was a tiny mouse, in Guildford, stuck in a cola can. And that Maggie, the young lady who had discovered this unhappy circumstance, was, although a self-professed animal lover, petrified of mice. Phobic, actually.

With no time to change – for fear of irreparable damage to either mouse or caller – I did an immediate about-turn and was back in the car and on the A3 in record time.

I have no idea what I must have looked like as, twenty minutes later, I stood on the lady's doorstep dressed in full black tie, clutching gloves, a carry case and a slender pair of wire cutters – 007: Wildlife Division, reporting for duty!

The door before me was suddenly flung open to reveal a woman in her – I would guess – mid-thirties, hopping from foot to foot with an expression nothing short of 'frantic' emitting from her terror-widened eyes. With no acknowledgement whatsoever of my bizarrely inappropriate attire, she jumped like a cat on a hot tin roof from hallway to doorstep and, scooting around behind me, cowered somewhere between my fine woollen (polyester) shoulder blades. By virtue of a mixture of shaking hands and words, I was ushered through the house and out the other side into a communal courtyard.

Goodness knows how – for the small concrete area was laden with litter – but immediately my gaze fell upon one particular cola can. As I watched, the can appeared to spasm, rolling forth a few inches and then resting. Leaving Maggie clinging on to the frame of her back door as if her life depended on it, I quietly approached the seemingly possessed Diet Coke.

With the aid of the courtyard's floodlight triggered by my presence, I was able to see better exactly what the little chap's predicament was.

Obviously enticed by the sweet smell of the sugary drink, the mouse had poked its head through the ring-pull-less opening on top of the discarded can. Burying in further and further to reach its syrupy prize, the youngster had become wedged, unable to go any further into the can due to the structural formation of its shoulders, but equally as incapable of reversing out past its unwilling ears.

Quickly realising that I would need the precision of the equipment available to me back at the centre to free this little mite, as gently as I possibly could, I picked up the whole ensemble and wrapped both mouse and can in one big towel, hoping that this manner of padding would stop the little one from squirming his way into further distress. Placing the towel-clad can and its occupant in an open cardboard box, I reached for my car keys.

I left Maggie with a double Scotch and, at her surprising request, the phone number of the Wildlife Aid hospital, so she could call the next morning to see how the patient was.

Back in the treatment room at the centre, I quickly put the mouse-in-the-can-in-the-towel-in-the-box ('I know an old lady who swallowed a fly...') into a big black bin liner, into which I ran a brief blast of anaesthetic gas. As soon as 'Hickorydickorydock' was unconscious, I set about laying him out on the operation table, whereupon I

211

carefully cut into the can with a small pair of surgical scissors. Once it was free, I examined the tiny patient and was relieved, if not astounded, to see that the can hadn't cut into the little one's skin at all!

Just as I had satisfied myself that there really was no damage whatsoever, the youngster – who could've been no more than 6–8 weeks old – began to show signs of coming round from his imposed slumber. I laid his twitching form softly on to a towel within one of the hospital's smaller incubators.

The following morning arrived to see a very active little wood mouse scurrying around the inside of his temporary home, unscathed and clearly still buzzing on a hazardously procured sugar high!

Hickorydickorydock (the smallest creature with the longest name!) was released into the large field that backs on to the centre later that day.

WOOD MOUSE FACT FILE

Name Wood mouse (*Apodemus sylvaticus*)
Class Mammalia
Order Rodentia
Family Muridae

Distribution (globally): Wood mice are found across Britain, Europe and Asia.

Habitat: Wood mice inhabit a large variety of places, such as woodlands, grasslands, farmlands, gardens and parks. They actually will inhabit most places as long as they are not too wet.

Size: They have a body length of between 8 and 11cm, with a tail length of 7–10cm.

Weight: 13–27g; they gain weight over the summer.

Description: Wood mice have reddish brown fur and a grey underbelly. They have large ears and a tail as long as their bodies.

Lifespan: Up to 20 months.

When most commonly seen: Wood mice are mainly nocturnal but do sometimes feed during the day. They do not hibernate, so are seen all year round.

Diet: Wood mice eat fruit, seeds, buds, insects, worms and fungi. They also eat soft faeces which they have already passed, to allow all nutrients to be absorbed a second time through their digestive system.

Reproduction facts: Breeding season begins in March and lasts through to October. A female may have 2 or more litters each year, even up to 7. A typical litter consists of 2–7 young. The gestation period last roughly 23 days. The young are weaned after about 18 days.

DID YOU KNOW?

Before mating, the male mice produce ultrasonic noises to soothe the female.

A wood mouse normally spends its life within an area of about 180m in diameter.

Although they do live in this small area, they may sometimes venture out at night, to areas where other small mammals will not go, travelling a distance of about 0.4km.

Past Walthamstow, Post Yard Arm

The Story of Billy-Ray the Polecat-Ferret

Now, as anyone who knows me will testify, I'm not a big drinker. I can't afford to be, owing to the fact that at any given moment I could be called out to drive to the scene of some wildlife incident or another.

But it had been an evening of rueful celebration. One of our most loved and respected, long-serving members of staff was flying Wildlife Aid's own proverbial nest for pastures new, and I admit (having of course first checked that the centre's emergency helpline was diverted from my mobile phone to that of another of our chief rescuers) that I had entered heartily into the spirit of the evening.

Waving off the last of my guests, I bolted the farmhouse door to the night and wandered through to the kitchen in search of something (although I was blowed if I could remember what). I flicked the switch on the kettle. Tea seemed like a plausible option. I leaned back on the kitchen counter and chatted to Jim as I waited (although I wasn't entirely clear on what exactly it was that I was waiting for).

'Aren't you going to answer that?' he asked me, gesturing to the sideboard.

Answer the kettle? Even in my merry state, frankly that seemed like a ridiculous notion.

Glancing in the direction of the kettle anyway, I noticed my mobile phone throwing itself around the surface (which amused me more than usual) in a bid to be heard. Rolling his eyes, Jim reached past me and picked up my phone. We were in the midst of filming the new series of *Wildlife SOS*, and our 24-hour callout service meant that it wasn't only I who had to be 'on duty' day and night, but also whichever cameraman was rota-bound to be present. This week it was Jim's turn.

'Right,' announced Jim, as he set my phone down on the table. 'That was Goff. He's over an hour away on a deer rescue, and there's a lady just north of Walthamstow who's found a polecat-ferret. It's bitten her quite badly, and she's insisting that someone be sent out to collect it tonight.'

'Right,' I said, waiting for Jim to continue. He didn't. 'Right,' I said again.

'I think we should go,' Jim offered. 'The polecat-ferret obviously needs collecting, and we're a bit short of stories forthe series.'

'Right.' I knew there were other words. I just couldn't think of them.

Putting my keys into the ignition, I turned to camera and announced where it was I was headed at such a late hour. Once my account of events had been recorded, I released the handbrake and allowed the car to roll forward a few feet – there was no way I was going to risk driving after a couple of glasses of wine – whereupon Jim downed his camera and I duly reinstated the handbrake so that he could drive us both to, um, wherever it was we were going.

As a surreal incidental to this particular night rescue, we had to make an unplanned stop en route to the polecat-ferret's recovery, at the unprecedented appearance before us of a dustbin lying abstractly in the middle of the road, seemingly pouring out fox cubs! (Had someone spiked the punch?) Notorious for their scavenging knack of upturning bins, one such canine chancer had seized an opportunity to do just that. After carefully steering the car into the side of the road, Jim leaped out to shepherd the vixen and her cubs back into the undergrowth, though they needed little encouragement, scattering at the first sniff of his presence. I watched then as he picked up the bin and placed it a good distance back from the road.

He glanced at me as he resumed his seat behind the wheel. 'Right,' I said in what I hoped was a decisive tone.

Soon we were pulling up the driveway of the Walthamstow address, and, following a quick passenger/driver seat swap, my arrival was filmed, and so too was my unfloodlit stumbling amble to the front door of number 12.

With his camera now trained on me as I stood on the doorstep, Jim said from behind the lens, 'Just quickly say why you're here.'

'Right.'

'And stop saying that!'

'Ri— OK.' I gave a brief explanation to camera as to the lady's polecat-ferret predicament, and rang the bell.

Eventually, after a commotion that had sounded worryingly like a violent burglary in progress, two ladies – probably in their late fifties and, I would suggest, slightly inebriated themselves – did not so much open the door as fall through it.

A ten-minute conversation ensued, which initially revealed that the pair had just returned from their line-dancing class (said class had actually finished several hours before, thus possibly accounting for their own irrepressibly 'spirited' joviality), and journeyed into an enthusiastic account of how they had come home to find the young polecat-ferret scratching at their door. Although distinctly informative, it was a sequence that would *never* make primetime television. Without even turning to meet his eye, I could feel Jim slowly losing the will to live.

'My colleague led me to believe you'd sustained quite a nasty injury as a result of handling your late-night caller,' I ventured in my most professional tone – mistakenly, as it transpired, because this had the ladies doubled over in hysterical laughter for its tenuous property of innuendo. Drying her eyes, one of the ladies poutily produced the index finger of her right hand – a padded drawing pin could have made more of an impression, I thought to myself.

Together, the four of us made our way out to the barn, where Esme and Trish had put the young polecat-ferret quietly in a box following Goff's earlier instruction. Poor Jim! He was faced with creating a 'rescue sequence' for *Wildlife SOS* out of precisely nothing – his three subjects ranged from 'merry' (me) to 'incoherent' (Trish), to the polecat-ferret ('pre-packaged')!

As I made to open the notably unstable box containing the polecat-ferret, Jim, in an attempt to add anything at all of note to the dubious tale, decided to conduct an impromptu interview.

'Where are polecat-ferrets from, Simon?'

My mind was blank.

'Where did it come from again?' I asked Esme.

'Walthamstow,' Trish stated proudly, if not a little loudly.

'Polecat-ferrets are from Walthamstow,' I declared (knowing that it didn't sound quite right).

As I peered in at the youngster, the first thing I couldn't really fail to notice was that it was dressed in a colourful little jacket and had a lead attached to its collar, instantly denoting that it was an escaped pet.

I reached in to pick up the youngster so that I could transfer it to my carry case, and, being not quite as dexterous as I should have been, procured myself a padded-drawing-pin wound of my very own, much to everyone's delight – especially Jim's.

Nursing one finger – now tightly wrapped in a flourescent-pink line-dancing scarf – I checked the young polecat-ferret over and, satisfied that it was entirely healthy, placed it in my carry case to take it back to the centre, where I would try to trace its owner or, failing that, re-home the youngster.

Politely declining the ladies' offers of coming in for a 'quick tipple', Jim and I hurriedly made our way back to the car.

223

Safely back at Wildlife Aid, the young polecat-ferret devoured a chick as if it hadn't eaten in weeks, before curling up to sleep.

Temporarily named 'Billy-Ray' by Esme and Trish, the youngster was collected first thing the next morning by his very relieved and very grateful owner.

POLECAT-FERRET FACT FILE

Name   European polecat (*Mustela putorius*)
Class   Mammalia
Order   Carnivora
Family Mustelidae
Terms   Male – hob; female – gill;
            young – kit

Distribution (globally): Polecat-ferrets inhabit large parts of Europe and Britain. There was a decline in numbers around Britain during the twentieth century. However, polecat-ferret populations are slowly growing again.

Habitat: Polecat-ferrets can be found mainly in forests, though they also live in marshlands, farmlands and sand dunes.

Size: Males have 40–50cm-long bodies; females are slightly shorter, growing to roughly 30–40cm. Their tails tend to be 10–20cm long.

Weight: 700g–1.5kg.

Description: Polecat-ferrets have slimline bodies, short legs, bushy tails, broad heads and small rounded ears. They have brown-black coats, with white markings on their faces.

Lifespan
In the wild: 4–5 years.
In captivity: Up to 14 years.

When most commonly seen: Polecat-ferrets are predominantly nocturnal animals, preferring to hunt at night. In the winter, they come out during the day more frequently than they do in the summer.

Diet: The polecat-ferret's main source of food is rabbits, small rodents and birds; they will also eat amphibians, birds' eggs and carrion.

Reproduction facts: Polecat-ferrets breed between March and June. The females usually produce only one litter a year; sometimes, however, they produce two. A typical litter consists of 5–10 young. The gestation period lasts around 42 days, and the kits are weaned after 4 weeks.

DID YOU KNOW?

In winter, the polecat-ferret's fur changes colour to a light grey, which provides a better camouflage.

A male polecat-ferret can control territories as large as 6,000 acres.

Polecat-ferrets are fierce hunters, and they can kill an animal almost twice their size. They also often kill animals without planning to eat them, when, for instance, they kill a whole rabbit litter only to eat one of the young.

A group of polecat-ferrets is called a business.

The Call of the Wild

The Story of the First Treecreepers

Back in the days when the sweets now called Starburst were still Opal Fruits (available in four distinct colours – red, orange, green and yellow only) and Snickers were still Marathons, Wildlife Aid's main centre of operation was My Kitchen – with supporting units housed in various other territories of my home, including the airing cupboard in my daughter's bedroom, the garden fish pond (which quickly became starkly devoid of any discernible fish) and my wife's 'fruit cage' (which, every bit as quickly, wound up utterly fruitless!).

My wife and I founded Wildlife Aid in 1980. Both of us had an innate inner calling to work in some way with animals, yet neither of us was

equipped with the necessary A-levels to become a vet. Over the years, time, the birth of our children, the consequent financial responsibility and life in general had led our shared vocational dream to elude us – until my parents retired, that is, moving out of the house that they had lived in for some forty years on the local farm that my father managed, and into the hastily prepared annexe that adjoined my property. Upon their arrival, I had to make notable renovations to my garden, namely the digging of a pond to accommodate the small menagerie of water foul that Dad had acquired during his years at the farm.

A matter of only days later, hearing that we had a pond and that my wife cared so much for all our furry and feathered friends, a lady turned up at our door with … A Cardboard Box – a sight that was to become very familiar indeed over the years that followed. Jill welcomed our visitor in and, over a cup of tea and a couple of chocolate digestives, listened to a concerned Anne's account of how she'd found the injured seagull and determined to bring it to 'the animal people's house on Randalls Road', in the hope that the poor wing-wounded creature could take solace under the shelter of Jill's own wing.

And so Wildlife Aid was born.

In the early days, still working in my city job, I

would come home of an evening to swap suit and briefcase for old clothes and a baby's bottle, whereupon I would immediately take up the next round of fox-cub feeds while Jill bathed the kids – completing the last pipette-served meal to the hoglets in the airing cupboard of Lou's bedroom over a Hans Christian Andersen tale as our tenderly aged eldest dozed off to sleep.

The very first weekend that I was officially 'on duty' saw me answering a dawn call. It was six o'clock in the morning and, having beaten my alarm clock to within an inch of its life, it slowly became apparent to me that my Saturday-morning lie-in was being denied to me not by my weekday-set alarm clock at all, but by the doorbell. Groggily ambling downstairs, I made my way to the front door.

The Cardboard Box, in this, my first shift, contained a squawking family of tiny nestlings. Resting the box on my 'examination table' (the chest freezer in the utility room), I peered in at the youngsters as their worried rescuer explained that her cat had brought in the mother of the now orphans, whom she'd got to in the nick of time, saving them from the same fate.

I jotted down the lady's details in the notebook that Jill had taped (suspended by what looked ominously like one of the laces from my work shoes) to the back door, and promised that I would call her later in the week to let her know how the young birds were doing.

Each morning on the train to London Waterloo, I had been earnestly reading any books on British wildlife and animal care that I could get my hands on. 'The birds need to be kept warm, dark and quiet,' I recited to myself. Right. Padding back into the kitchen with The Cardboard Box, I surveyed the room for possible options. Oven? Dark, quiet, but possibly a bit too warm! Kitchen counter? Too noisy – the kids would be up soon. Hmm. Setting the nestlings down on the table, for want of a better idea, I opened the nearest cupboard. Saucepans, saucepans, saucepans. Electric frying pan! Brilliant! Like a child with a new train set, I eagerly wrenched the pan from the back of the cupboard, bringing with it the rest of the cupboard's content in an ear-splitting symphony of discordant mayhem. The kids would definitely be up now. Oh well. I had important animal-saving work to do!

I hurried into the lounge and, in one deft move, swept the entire surface of coffee-table clutter flying indiscriminately to the floor. Plugging the electric pan into the mains, I painstakingly gently lifted the whole nest from box to pan and switched the archaic device over to its 'on' position – opting, with the assistance of my pyjama'd youngest, for 'very low simmer' out of a possible 'warm', 'reheat' and 'roast'. Pleased with my work (and selectively oblivious to the domestic chaos in its wake), I scribbled a note to Jill, and rushed out to my car.

It turns me inside out with embarrassment now to imagine what I must have looked like to the proprietor of the local fishing-tackle shop: a grown man, beating down his door at seven o'clock in the morning, in seemingly life-threatening need of fresh maggots. In his dressing gown. And one slipper.

The orphaned birds thrived, cared for meticulously by Jill and me, who were following the orders of every bit of literature ever written on the subject of such matters, to the letter.

Watching our first youngsters, a family of healthy young treecreepers, fly the nest weeks later was a truly humbling yet proud moment. The fact that we actually believed they were robins for the duration of their time with us is neither here nor there(!)

TREECREEPER FACT FILE

Name Treecreeper (*Certhia familiaris*)
Class Aves
Order Passeriformes
Family Certhiidae

Distribution (globally): Treecreepers are found across most of Britain and Europe. They are also found in Northern and Central Asia.

Habitat: Treecreepers inhabit woodlands, parks, gardens, most places with mature trees.

Size: They grow to about 12cm back to tail, with a wingspan of 17–21cm.

Weight: 8–11g.

Description: Treecreepers have white underparts; the rest of their plumage is a brown, speckled colour. They have long, slender, downward-pointing beaks.

Lifespan: Up to 8 years.

When most commonly seen: Treecreepers

can be seen all year round, though are seen more often during the autumn and winter months.

Diet: Mainly small insects and beetles. However, during the winter, they will eat various seeds as well.

Reproduction facts: Courting begins in early April, and the breeding season lasts until July. The female usually lays 5–6 eggs, which are incubated for about 2 weeks before hatching. The young remain in the nest for only a further 2 weeks, before leaving to live separately.

DID YOU KNOW?

Treecreepers are not strong fliers. They often simply flutter from the top of one tree to the next.

The treecreeper was first recorded in Britain around 900 years ago.

Much like a woodpecker, the treecreeper also uses its tail feathers as a prop when climbing trees.

The treecreeper makes a high-pitched 'tsee-tsee' call, which is often confused with the noise of a mouse.

Afterword

I hope that you have enjoyed this book and that it has given you some insight into the lighter side of our work and what we, the staff and the volunteers of Wildlife Aid, go through on a day-to-day basis – the scares, the sadness, the disappointments as well as the joys and the spiritual rewards of caring for wild creatures.

If there's a theme running through this book, then I guess it's about survival – often against the odds. Our work at Wildlife Aid is challenging, exhilarating and fulfilling – we wouldn't do it otherwise! But there is also sadness when our patients don't pull through, or when there's simply nothing we can do to help.

The biggest challenge facing us now, however, is

whether Wildlife Aid itself will remain financially sustainable. When the charity was set up, a quarter of a century ago, I had no idea that it would grow to become one of Britain's leading wildlife charities.

But here we are today: we have a state-of-the-art veterinary hospital and a rehabilitation centre that costs us over a quarter of a million pounds every year to maintain. We have full-time veterinary nurses and on-call vets, backed up by hundreds of volunteers; and, on top of that, we're on TV every week in *Wildlife SOS* – now Britain's longest-running and most popular wildlife documentary series.

And to think it all started in my kitchen!

In all, we deal with well over 12,000 wildlife incidents every year – but these patients don't have medical insurance and can't write us a cheque after we've treated them! And there's no taxpayers' money to bail us out.

Every penny of the £260,000 we spend each year on hospital equipment, medicines, supplies and the ongoing running costs of the Wildlife Aid centre, comes from private donations, membership subscriptions, fundraising schemes and the occasional donation from a philanthropic company or charitable institution. However, we also desperately need legacies, as these are so vital in supporting most charities.

Due to continual price increases (especially for pharmaceutical supplies, and other essentials such as petrol and maintenance for our emergency rescue vehicles), our core costs are running way ahead of the money that's coming in and we have to draw on our reserves to keep the charity afloat.

The vital plans we made a few years back for the expansion of the hospital, its relocation to more suitable premises and the addition of a much-needed wildlife education centre as part of the complex, have had to be put on hold.

But wouldn't it be wonderful if, as well as continuing our work – 'actively caring for British wildlife', as it says under our logo – we were also able to do something tangible to educate others about the nation's wildlife and to play an even greater role in helping to redress the terrible imbalance between Man and Nature?

We have battled away on behalf of the 'silent majority' – Britain's wild animals – for 25 years. We're not about to disappear. This is too important a mission for any of us involved in the front line of this battle just to give up and go home.

But the struggle is getting tougher by the day. We desperately need more money – to keep the charity going and to enable us to move forward to the next stage of Wildlife Aid's development.

We can help our wildlife, if you will help us.

Simon

About Wildlife Aid

Wildlife Aid is a registered charity (No. 297610) dedicated to the rescue, care and rehabilitation of sick, injured and orphaned wild animals. The charity has a fully equipped veterinary hospital in Leatherhead, Surrey, and an emergency rescue service that deals with some 12,000 wildlife casualties every year. Wildlife Aid operates mainly in the southeast of England but provides advice and a referral service for wildlife emergencies throughout the UK.

As we've seen, the work of Wildlife Aid is the subject of the popular television series *Wildlife SOS*. Members of Wildlife Aid receive the regular magazine *Wildlife Aid in Action*, a membership certificate and discounted admission to the charity's annual open day. The charity also runs a successful Adopt-an-Animal scheme.

To find out how to help the charity's work, write to:

Simon Cowell MBE
Wildlife Aid
Randalls Farmhouse
Randalls Road
Leatherhead
Surrey
KT22 0AL

Telephone 01372 377332 (ask for membership).

For animal enquiries, please call 09061 800132 (calls charged at 50p per minute).

Or visit our website: http://www.wildlifeaid.com.